361   Simpson, C. & D.
Sim   Careers in Social
       Work

DATE	ISSUED TO

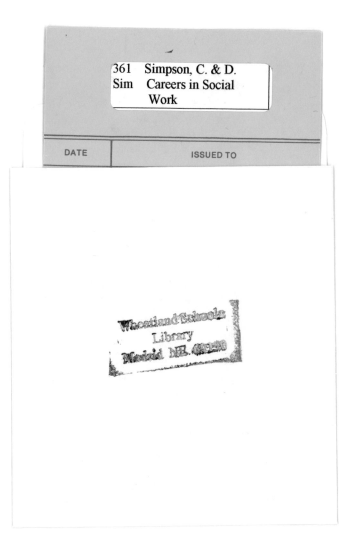

CAREERS IN
SOCIAL WORK

By
CAROLYN SIMPSON AND
DWAIN SIMPSON

The Rosen Publishing Group, Inc.
NEW YORK

Published in 1992, 1994, 1996, 1999 by The Rosen Publishing Group, Inc.
29 East 21st Street, New York, NY 10010

Revised Edition 1999

Library of Congress Cataloging-in-Publication Data

Simpson, Carolyn.
    Careers in social work / by Carolyn Simpson and Dwain Simpson.
        p.   cm.
    Includes bibliographical references and index.
    Summary: A discussion of the career opportunities in social work, how to get involved, where to get more information, and how to prepare for a career in this area.
    ISBN 0-8239-2879-9 (hc)
    1. Social service—Vocational guidance—United States—Juvenile literature. [1. Social service—Vocational guidance. 2. Vocational guidance.] I. Simpson, Dwain, 1951-   . II. Title.
HV10.5.S56   1992
361.3'2'02373 - dc20   91-14457
                                                                          CIP
                                                                           AC

Manufactured in the United States of America

About the Authors

Carolyn Simpson has worked in the mental-health field since 1973. She received a BA degree from Colby College in Waterville, Maine, and an MA from the University of Oklahoma in Norman, Oklahoma.

Over the years, she has worked in a variety of social work capacities: as an intern with the Department of Human Services, as a clinical social worker in Maine and Oklahoma, and as a school counselor in an alternative program in Bridgton, Maine.

Currently she is an outpatient therapist at Parkside Behavioral Health Services in Tulsa, Oklahoma. She also teaches psychology at Tulsa Community College.

Dwain Simpson is a licensed clinical social worker and the outpatient clinic director at Tulsa Regional Medical Center Behavioral Health Services, Tulsa, Oklahoma. He is also in private practice.

He has worked as a clinical social worker since 1977, and has held jobs in Maine and Oklahoma. He received both a BA and an MSW from the University of Oklahoma, Norman.

The Simpsons have collaborated on two other books: *Coping with Emotional Disorders* (which discusses the problems in adolescence requiring some form of mental-health treatment) and *Coping with Post-Traumatic Stress Disorder.* They live with their three children on the outskirts of Tulsa.

Acknowledgments

Special thanks to Sondra Shehab LCSW/BCD, our friend and colleague in Norman, Oklahoma, for her help with this revision.

We are also indebted to several others who helped us with this newest edition. Many thanks to Gary Blank, LCSW and Michelle Blank, LCSW, Angie Bauer, MSW, and Marcy McMurry, MSW, who went to great lengths to provide material. Special thanks once again to Belinda Posey who researched the schools offering the MSW program.

Contents

Introduction:
Common Misconceptions
About Social Workers

Every semester I get a new crop of students in my Human Relations class, and every semester I hear the same old misconceptions. In fact, I encourage them to bring these misconceptions out into the open; that's the only way to dispel them. Here's how I start: I ask my students to think of certain occupations and try to imagine what kind of car a person working in that profession might drive.

"How about a lawyer?" I ask.

"Easy," someone says. "A Lexus."

"Or a BMW," another adds.

They are clearly warming to the task.

"How about a doctor?" I ask.

"Same thing," someone says.

"Well, it depends on if he's retired. Then he'd probably have a Cadillac," another says.

So far, my students aren't bothering to question whether the lawyer and doctor are women, whether they're successful, or where they live.

"How about a banker?" I ask.

"Is he the president of the bank, or a loan officer?" one student says.

Now they're catching on. Most people base their assumptions on their assessment of the jobs themselves. A president would make more money than a loan officer, and so would drive a more expensive car.

1

"What about a social worker?" I ask. No one knows my background, nor that my husband is a social worker.

Several people snicker. "Probably a Ford Escort," one says.

"Or one of those old Saabs with the hubcaps coming off," another adds.

"Wait a minute," I say. (I have nothing against Ford Escorts and old Saabs, but clearly these students are picking inexpensive—even old and shabby—cars for social workers to own.) "What makes you think social workers drive inexpensive cars?"

"Because they don't make much money," someone says.

"Besides, what social worker would want to drive her husband's brand new Buick around the poor part of town?" another asks.

"What makes you think social workers are all women driving their cars around in the poor part of town?" I ask.

"You know," one says. "Social workers and welfare: the two go together."

So begins another semester. Most of my students have no idea what social workers do other than distribute welfare checks and check on foster kids.

COMMON MISCONCEPTIONS

Because so many people have the wrong idea (or at least a limited perspective) of what social workers do and who they are, we're going to discuss a few of the common misconceptionss.

1. All social workers drive economy cars because:
   a. They're women.
   b. They're underpaid.
   c. They're driving around checking on welfare clients.

Not all social workers drive economy cars; in fact, some drive expensive sports cars, minivans, and pickup trucks. Some even have motorcycles, and many do drive economy cars (but that's more a sign of the times).

People make these assumptions because they assume that social workers are women, and women are notoriously underpaid. Actually, the number of men and women in social work jobs depends on the specific type of social work position. Women do seem to fill the more traditional social work positions, in part because these jobs have more flexible hours and work-leave policies. (That's a consideration when you're raising a family.) Men seem to fill more administrative positions and the less traditional jobs. In general, men can move more easily up the ladder of success, so you often find a disproportionate number of males in the higher-paying jobs.

Women often find themselves underpaid. Anyone performing a job considered "women's work" has the same complaint, so it's not surprising that people think all social workers are underpaid. Actually, it's only the traditional social work positions that don't pay well. Administrative positions and many clinical social work positions pay extremely well.

Finally, social workers do a lot more than check on their welfare clients. Some provide family-planning services, some provide therapy (both in inpatient and outpatient settings), and others run organizations or form the core of crisis intervention teams.

This just goes to show that you can't judge all social workers by the one job you usually associate with social workers.

2. Social workers are limited in what they do.

That's one of the biggest misperceptions today. In fact, social workers have one of the most versatile degrees, the Master of Social Work (MSW) degree. They can

3

teach. They can write up grants and organize community projects, as well as work in more traditional jobs with welfare recipients and foster-care providers. They can provide counseling services. As a matter of fact, social workers are the primary providers of mental-health services: they provide more therapy than psychologists or psychiatrists. Insurance companies prefer to reimburse social workers because they charge less than psychologists and essentially do the same work. The only things limiting social workers are their aspirations.

Furthermore, the National Association of Social Workers (NASW) is a formidable lobbying group in Washington.

3. Social workers lead dull and boring lives.

The only people who make this assumption are people who have never been social workers. Social work is many things—exhausting, challenging, discouraging, and gratifying—but it is never dull or boring. Social workers work with people, and people are always different. Depending on their positions, some social workers lead more exciting lives than others. Crisis intervention workers specialize in emergencies; they may jet all over the world to help survivors cope with traumatic experiences. Some social workers join the Peace Corps and travel to Africa and Asia to work in Third World countries. Adapting to a whole new culture can hardly be called boring.

AN OVERVIEW OF THIS BOOK

We begin with a history of social work to give you an idea why it has been considered "women's work" and why it has been underpaid for so long. Relative to other professions, social work is a new profession (although "helpers" have been around tending to others since the dawn of man).

4

The people best suited to social work are not necessarily the students with the best grades in school. Resourcefulness, a sensitivity to others' needs, and initiative are far more useful qualities to possess.

This book discusses the educational requirements for social work and how to pick a good college for this field. In the past, you could get just about any degree in the mental-health field and then practice social work; that is no longer possible. The BSW (Bachelor in Social Work) is just a starting point now. Unless you go on and earn the MSW, you will not qualify for many positions. Many people are now getting their DSW (Doctor of Social Work) or PhD in Social Work because those are stronger credentials. Social workers can now be board certified in their clinical work (which adds impressive credentials to their name), but only if their graduate program offers the right courses to qualify them for the rigorous national exam. We have information on board certification.

The bulk of the book examines specific social work jobs, detailing the salaries, the good and bad points, the opportunities, and how to break into the field. We conclude with some other career opportunities closely related to the social work profession; you might be surprised at the other kinds of work you can do with a background in social work.

LOOKING TOWARD THE NEW MILLENNIUM . . .

The nineties have brought new opportunities and problems to social workers. Those who provide clinical services, both inpatient and outpatient therapy, have to consider the effects of managed care. In the past, a clinical social worker (otherwise known as therapist) could develop a long-term relationship with a client, reporting only a diagnosis and a brief description of services rendered to the client's insurance company. With the advent of managed care, social workers often have to change to short-term therapy skills (sometimes called "solution-focused" therapy). When social workers work for a provider of an HMO (Health Maintenance Organization), the focus of their work shifts from developing a long-term supportive relationship with the client to helping solve the immediate problem at hand. Even if a social worker is in private practice, he or she still has to deal with third-party reimbursement (insurance companies that are footing the bill). Insurance companies (along with HMOs) dictate how many sessions (and what problems) they will cover. Needless to say, many therapists are turned off by this level of involvement by third-party handlers.

If you're interested in providing clinical services, you need to realize that you'll be seeing more clients than others have in the past, and you'll constantly be focusing on meeting treatment objectives. The sheer volume of clients as well as the need to get authorization for treatment from insurance companies can be discouraging. Although the focus is on cost efficiency and productivity, don't lose sight of your main task: providing quality therapy in a solution-focused manner. Managed care seems to be a fixture of the nineties, like it or not. Those who can adapt will find plenty of work.

Crisis intervention work presents an exciting new opportunity for social workers. Social workers (trained to handle trauma victims as well as their rescuers) travel to on-site locations to deal with the survivors of catastrophes. Social workers deal with the victims of mass shootings, victims of fires, earthquakes, hurricanes, and tornadoes. A recent example of this was the explosion of the Alfred Murrah federal building in Oklahoma City in 1995. More than 168 people were killed and hundreds more were injured. Many social workers were called upon to help survivors and families of victims.

Finally, social workers now have the opportunity to train to be psychoanalysts without becoming doctors first. A lawsuit in the late 1980s successfully challenged the American Psychological Society for restricting psychoanalytic training to psychiatrists. This has opened up an entirely new area to social workers (who need no more than an MSW to enter training). Several institutes offer psychoanalytic training. If you're interested in a specific program, you need to find out the specific requirements. In general, psychoanalytic training consists of a five-year program set up so that people can work as well as attend classes. Tuition is approximately $2,400 a year. The student must also supply a supervisor (who acts as a case consultant) and must engage in personal analysis for a year and a half. The purpose of analysis is to learn the process first hand by being analyzed yourself, and to keep your problems and issues from interfering with those of your clients. Analysis is expensive (upward of $100 an hour) and comes out of the student's own pocket. The cost is deductible, however, as part of the training. Over the five-year period, the student handles three psychoanalytic cases under supervision.

Even if you're not interested in becoming a psychoanalyst (the costs would not be covered under a managed care plan), you may discover that your regular therapy skills are enhanced by the knowledge of psychoanalytic priniciples.

Heading to the new millennium means more opportunities for social workers. Traditional social work is giving way to more "business-like" jobs, and that will be the subject of the first chapter.

More in-depth exploration of jobs, including several new ones, takes place in Part II of this book. And finally, this newest revision offers a degree listing at the back of the book of colleges in the United States offering the MSW.

PART I

THE WORLD OF SOCIAL WORK

1

Social Work in the New Millennium

As the end of the century (and millennium) draws close, different social work opportunities present themselves. You have already read that insurance companies and Health Maintenance Organizations (HMOs) are changing the way medical services and psychotherapy are being delivered. Hospitals, mental-health centers, and social workers in private practice are all required to call the insurance providers of those with insurance to get approval for specific services before any services are delivered.

Who approves or denies the services being requested? Most insurance companies hire licensed mental-health professionals (preferably social workers) to fill this role because they have some understanding of those needing the services.

A social worker whose job is to authorize or deny services that the insurance company will pay for has to have knowledge of the services being requested and the client's particular illness. So, someone interested in this kind of work would be wise to work first as a medical social worker or a therapist.

Because of the growing influence of insurance companies, there will always be demand for knowledgeable social workers to authorize services. Depending on the company and the state you live in, the pay can vary from $25,000 a year to $35,000. The social worker has a varied workday (never knowing who will call in to request services or extension of services). He or she spends the day:

- Authorizing and reauthorizing specific services once the person requesting the service makes it clear why it is needed
- Attending hospital team meetings to learn why extensions of services might be needed
- Accounting to the insurance companies to keep costs down

Another market that is, unfortunately, booming is the corrections department's need for clinical social workers. The number of criminals being incarcerated these days is increasing, so social workers will always have a job helping the emotionally disturbed in prison. (See chapter 13 for an in-depth discussion of this job.)

The media have brought to our attention the incidence of violence in our schools, and the schools' attempts to deal with it. As weapons remain so available to teenagers, and frustrated teens are so quick to use them to solve problems, schools are now looking to professionals to introduce conflict resolution skills to their students.

Here is another job opportunity for social workers who like to work with kids. Conflict resolution courses abound and many schools are now contracting with mental-health agencies to provide these skills to their students.

Finally, the fact that the baby boomers have reached middle age means that there will be an increasing need for people to work with this aging population. Social workers will be needed to provide hospice care and to work in nursing homes in the not so distant future (keeping aging baby boomers in touch with their families, keeping their minds stimulated, and their spirits up).

Depending on whether or not a cure for AIDS is found soon, there will be plenty of opportunities to work with people who have AIDS. As people live longer lives, but not necessarily better-quality lives, there will continue to be a need for social workers to provide their services: case management, individual therapy, and family therapy. Social workers will always be in demand. Hopefully, as society realizes the importance of their work, social workers' salaries will rise.

A Historical Perspective

Throughout the ages people have donned the cap of social worker—helping their neighbor in time of need. But in the beginning, social work was not a bona fide profession. Social workers were simply people in the community who did "good deeds." And they were not paid for them. Two significant events changed all that: the Industrial Revolution and urbanization. When the United States started to change from an agricultural country into an industrial nation, people flocked to the cities for jobs, abandoning the farms. Immigrants poured in from their homelands and settled in run-down city tenements. People who in the past had relied on their huge families to work the farms found themselves saddled with too many mouths to feed.

Subsequent poverty, unemployment, and an increasing number of immigrants who did not understand the ways of urban society led to greater social disorganization. In the past the mentally ill person, the pauper, and the criminal were all handled in the community. In the anonymity of the cities, state government groups arose to deal with them. Other watchdog groups followed to see that the socially disadvantaged were treated appropriately.

Two sets of people sprang from these circumstances—one set who wanted to find ways to help the needy, and another set who theorized about the causes of and solutions to the new problems. The two groups, with their conflicting views of "the problem," joined together to form the American Social Science Association (ASSA) in 1865. Still, these people could not agree on the appropriate focus for their work—should they work to change the causes of the problems or should they concentrate on treating persons beset by poverty, poor sanitation, and joblessness? One group became the workers, and the other remained tied to their theories, trying to pinpoint environmental causes of poverty with a view to reform. The "doers" and the "thinkers" could not get along. Finally, in 1874, the work segment of the group withdrew and formed the Conference of Charities, which later became the National Conference of Charities and Corrections (NCCC).

Two people who lent support to the social work movement were Dorothea Dix and Jane Addams. Dorothea Dix began her work in the mid-1800s, volunteering to teach Sunday school for prison inmates. What she discovered in 1841 was that the mentally ill prisoners were housed alongside the criminals, with no provision made for treating their illnesses. Dorothea Dix spent the rest of her life lobbying for improved prison conditions for the mentally ill.

Jane Addams was concerned with the poor, and especially the children, who lived in the slums of the cities. She knew that their housing was inadequate, that play space was nonexistent, and that the residents resorted to burglary and delinquency because there was not enough food to go around nor enough jobs to keep the adults fruitfully occupied.

Initially, people had viewed the "afflicted" person as someone who was "morally weak" and had brought on all of his or her problems, including sickness, unemployment, and poverty. The prevailing attitude of "You get what you deserve" derived from the Puritan work ethic. Good people worked hard; lazy people didn't, and that supposedly explained the appalling conditions of poverty intermixed with the affluence of other neighborhoods.

The charity services that sprang up in the 1880s were often run by well-to-do, educated young women who felt good about "doing something for the needy." Affluent community members gave freely as well, in part because they saw their giving of alms as a way to "enter the Kingdom of Heaven." They looked down on the people they helped. They saw themselves as superior because they had the money and position in the community not to need assistance.

The people who set up the first settlement houses had a different philosophy. They believed that what truly helped people of misfortune was "good neighboring." Giving charity to people only embarrassed them; what really helped was giving them knowledge—the means by which they could eventually help themselves. In settlement houses the "social workers" moved into the community. Once the people realized that the person was "one of them," they were receptive to the help offered.

Jane Addams lived a privileged life until she decided, after graduating from college, to pursue a lifelong goal of helping others in the city slums. She purchased a mansion in Chicago and settled in with some colleagues. At first she had only a vague idea of how she would help the neighbors. She did not want to patronize them. The neighbors, however, ended up telling her what they needed most. The day after they moved into the mansion a young mother appeared on the doorstep with two children huddled beside her. The mother asked if Jane and her colleagues would watch her children for a while because the sitter had not arrived that day, and the mother couldn't risk being late to work. Jane Addams welcomed the children and even invited the mother to breakfast. Within a matter of days, other neighbors brought their children, too, and Jane's home, Hull mansion (now called Hull House), offered its first service—day care. Jane Addams was remarkably gifted in attracting people with the skills she needed to help out at Hull House. Soon a kindergarten teacher was hired to run the day-care class for the children.

From day care, Jane Addams branched out into social clubs (a popular idea among settlement houses and adopted from the English), because she found she could reach more people not by preaching to them, but by providing a place to meet and exchange ideas. Because of the huge immigrant population, she encouraged the sharing of cultures; the neighborhood children could feel proud of their parents and build on their identities, despite the changes their families faced in this new country. The social clubs also presented the "American way of life" in a less threatening way. The residents learned how to cook nutritious meals and how to read and speak English. And because of the exchange of ideas they were able to contribute something of themselves. The settlement houses allowed—in fact encouraged—the neighbors to give back to others. "Giving back" kept them from feeling inferior and in need of charity.

Jane Addams's Hull House enjoyed a long history. Because of her "good neighboring," settlement houses sprang up in other cities such as Boston and New York. Jane Addams established the first public park for children in Chicago, improved the sanitation of the city, and encouraged the residents to take pride in their dwellings. She lobbied for safer working conditions and better schools. But more than that, she helped raise immigrants' self-esteem by valuing each person's past and helping that person fit into the present. In recognition of her lifelong achievements, Jane Addams received the Nobel Peace Prize in 1931. She was the first American woman to win the honor.

Settlement houses played an important role in social reform until after World War I, when the movement lost its momentum. Workers in these settlement houses joined the National Conference on Social Welfare (of which Jane Addams was the first female president), and they began to think of themselves as a professional group—social workers.

At the same time, charity organizations were also developing. The charity organizations believed in giving to the poor and needy, but to do so properly they wanted to come up with ways to document the need for their services. That meant visiting the homes, witnessing the client's need, and then returning to the office to record what service was needed. Wanting to soften their stance somewhat by being "neighborly" too, they called these people "friendly visitors." Unfortunately, helpful as they were, they focused only on solving the person's problems one at a time and made no effort to change the conditions that might have caused the predicament.

Friendly visitors were at first volunteers: again, young, well-educated females. Gradually, as the volunteers were replaced by paid workers, the "social workers" saw a need to connect themselves to a college to lend some professionalism to their ranks. In 1898, the charity organizations created the first school of philanthropy, which eventually became Columbia University School of Social Work. Some newly developed schools of social work emphasized apprenticeship programs so the workers could put into practice what they learned in classes. Other schools wanted more emphasis on theory and academics so that the world would view social workers as professionals. (Until then the average citizen couldn't be sure just what social workers did—or were licensed to do.) Having an advanced degree in social work suggested that this was now a bona fide profession.

Social work focused on three major areas. The casework method focused on services for the individual (but some said it neglected the interplay of environmental factors). The second area—group work—arose from the social clubs of the settlement era and proved useful in restructuring community life. The American Association of Group Workers was created in 1946 and became the National Association of Social Workers (NASW) in 1956.

The third area of focus was organizational social work, as social workers looked toward implementing, coordinating, and changing existing services in agencies as a whole.

The 1970s saw the emptying out of the psychiatric hospitals into the communities. This impetus was based on the belief that it was far more humane to have the mentally ill remain in the community as much as possible. Unfortunately, patients who had been hospitalized for thirty years were not equipped to handle life outside the hospital. Likewise, communities were fearful of the "strange-acting" former patients and didn't want them roaming their streets or living in nearby boarding homes. This longstanding tension created a need for social workers to facilitate the adjustment of both the former patients to the community and the community to the patients. Area businesses hired social workers to act as liaisons between the business community and the mental-health agencies.

Relatively speaking, social work is a new profession. Social workers continue to struggle with their identity. In the recent past, people from other academic disciplines such as sociology, psychology, or education could wear the "social worker's hat," and there was no real way to monitor the profession. Now that NASW is defining who can call themselves social workers (and only those who have earned a specific degree in social work, such as the BSW, MSW, or DSW can do so), more and more people are in agreement about the focus of treatment—not just the individual, but his whole system: his family interaction, his environment, and other factors.

Social workers occupy a variety of positions in the community. They work in hospitals helping people link up with the resources they will need when they are discharged. They work in private business, either assisting employers and employees in settling work-related disputes, or organizing new programs to assist management. They work in psychiatric settings, much as psychologists do, and some have built prestigious careers from their workshops and writings. Some social workers assume supervisory roles; some work with prison inmates; some arrange adoptions and foster-home placements. Some counsel young adults on reproductive issues; some work in the schools to intervene with troubled students. Some social workers teach other social workers, and if they teach in major universities they have the potential to make six-figure salaries. Other social workers choose to fight the system and make lasting changes in the environment; although they are not paid much to do it, they receive tremendous satisfaction. Social workers are in the military and the Peace Corps, in recreation groups for children, and in hospices for the terminally ill.

Qualities for Success

Before we consider what qualities you need for social work, let's look at why people want to go into social work in the first place. I have already told you it is not a money-making profession. Most social workers make a modest living (although some are able to earn more by going into private practice or teaching at the college level). If you don't go into social work for the money, why *do* you go into it? Obviously you must have some compelling reason to do work that is sometimes dangerous, sometimes stressful, and not always well rewarded.

Before we go any further, let me tell you something about helping people. Needy people do not like needing help. Most people do not appreciate handouts; they feel at a disadvantage. The social worker's job, then, is to lend a helping hand without increasing the dependence of the recipient at the same time. Sometimes you have to take a good, hard look at your motives before you can be any real help to people. You do not go into social work to feel better about your station in life. You have to feel some connection to these other people, and you have to believe that they have something to teach you too.

If you asked a random group of people in the helping professions why they selected this type of work—and if they responded honestly—you would probably find that more than 50 percent wanted to learn more about themselves.

By studying the human mind, by helping others face adversity, you learn things that you can use. Nothing is wrong with entering the profession to help heal your own problems, as long as you remember that to be effective you must be healthier than the client, and you cannot rely on him or her to help you.

Many people will tell you that they have gone into the profession because it is gratifying work. Why is it gratifying? Is it because they think other people need them? Is it because they happen to have skills that apply to the work?

Some people are not certain why they enter the field. One man became interested in clinical social work after being assigned to a psychiatric hospital in his first-year field placement. Until then he had not been sure what he wanted to do.

A college friend who is now a psychologist could not decide whether to pursue psychology or drama. She took courses in both subjects, but was unable to make up her mind. Finally, she sought out one of her favorite professors after class and asked his advice. She told him she was equally interested in both fields.

"What should I do?" she asked. She expected a lecture, a plan.

The professor reached into his pocket and pulled out a coin. Without explaining further, he shoved the coin across the desk to her and said, "Flip it."

"What for?" my friend asked.

"Heads, you go into drama. Tails, you go on in psychology."

"You're kidding," she said. "That's it? That's your plan?"

She looked at the coin and then back at him. "But what if it comes up drama?" she asked, and it wasn't until that moment that she knew there was really only one choice.

People in the helping professions who are the most effective choose to help people because they are good at it. You get satisfaction from doing what you do well.

So let's look at the qualities possessed by people who are most effective in the helping professions—qualities that would be useful even as a student.

Because your work brings you into contact with people every day, you need the ability to get along with others. More than just getting along, you need to like people, because people seeking your help may sense insincerity. Chances are if you like someone you'll want to help him or her grow, not become dependent on the services you offer.

Working well with people means that you have good social skills. If you do not know how to conduct yourself in public, you should take your cues from someone who does. Your image is important, and whether you choose to be or not, you will be a role model for many clients. One often learns by example, not from specific advice. (If maturity and good manners are not your strong points, don't despair. A crash course in job and social skills is featured in the last chapter.)

It is not enough to be sociable; you must also be able to handle angry people—people who may not want your help in the first place. First, learn to handle your own feelings—particularly anger—because you must be calm and reasonable when others are not. If you are ruled by your emotions, you will be as unpredictable as the people you are supposed to be helping. Anger is energizing—it's not all bad—so it is a good tool as long as you can channel it constructively.

Social workers have been called diplomats at times. You learn early on that there are times to take a stand and times to stand back. You may already possess these skills. Are you good at settling disputes between your friends? Do people look to you for a fair assessment of their problems?

Initiative is another necessary quality, because in some jobs you will find yourself given little direction and great leeway. You may be the only social worker in your area or department, and it will be up to you to finish your paperwork on time, manage your caseload, and respond to crises as they occur. If you need someone to tell you what to do every minute of the day, this will be a hard job for you. You must be the type of person who can decide just what needs to be done that day or down the line. Part of initiative is anticipating need, and that means thinking ahead and being prepared. Think about it. Are you the type of person who needs a lot of direction to finish a school project, or can you work independently?

Anyone with initiative may also be compulsive. The more "polite" term is organized, and if organization is not your strong suit either, don't worry. That is an area you can improve on, and I'll show you ways in the next chapter.

When I started working as a social worker in a private psychiatric hospital, I was overwhelmed on the first day with paperwork, a heavy caseload, and a list of rules. The other two workers were psychologists, and although they had been there a few weeks they were also overwhelmed. At the end of the first week when I turned in my paperwork on time, my boss praised me—and my colleagues groaned. They were still a week behind. Later, I took them aside and apologized for making them feel less competent. "It's just that I'm a compulsive person," I said. "Social work has taught me to organize my time and to make peace with paperwork."

If you are to work independently, you must learn to organize your time and to establish priorities.

Otherwise you'll be staring at a mountain of paperwork and working evenings to catch up.

Sallie is a medical social worker who is also the director of her department. She may go for weeks at a time without seeing another social worker because they are all assigned to separate wings of the hospital. Sallie cannot schedule her day because she covers the emergency room, and everyone knows that it is subject to surprising and varied accidents. Sallie demonstrates another trait of the successful social worker: independence. Independence and initiative go hand in hand. You have to be independent (and autonomous) to handle the isolation that you may feel working separately from other social workers. And you need initiative to know what to do with your time when you spend so much of it without guidance.

When I started as a psychiatric social worker in a hospital in Maine, the clinical director gave me a brief orientation to their services and the paperwork. That instruction lasted two hours on a Saturday morning. When I arrived on Monday no one greeted me at the door. Instead, word had been left at the front desk for me to come up to the floor and begin work. I remember walking into the nurse's station and saying, "I'm here."

A nurse pointed to names in blue chalk on the blackboard. "Those are your patients," she said.

"That's it?" I asked. "What you do want me to do?"

"Whatever it is that social workers do," the nurse answered.

Fortunately, I had been around hospitals long enough to know what I was supposed to do. The inexperienced social worker might be in for a shock.

It is not enough to be independent and self-starting; you must also be resourceful. That does not mean being a walking encyclopedia of resources. It simply means that you must know where to look for help, because most of the time you will be the one responsible for finding that help.

People learn early to be resourceful. Are you able to find a store that sells a vintage rookie baseball card when your friends swear it doesn't exist? Are you enough of a quick thinker that when your parents say, "If you earn $500, we'll foot the rest of the cost for a car," you can come up with the money within a couple of months? That's resourcefulness.

Successful social workers can carry on conversations with people while also stockpiling information for future resources. If you have to help a homeless person find transportation back to Iowa, it helps to know a few organizations that have funds for that kind of situation. If you meet with a family who can no longer look after Aunt Eunice because they work during the day and she has started wandering the streets looking for them, it helps to know what to do with Aunt Eunice during the day.

If you are dependent on writing grant proposals to fund your latest project (as community organizers do), you have to be resourceful at *finding* the money when the economy is tight. If you work in a business setting, you have to be both diplomatic and resourceful to smooth over labor disputes. Diplomatic, because touchy situations call for finesse; resourceful, because often the solutions are not waiting around to be discovered.

The next quality required is harder to describe. It is the ability to recognize and maintain boundaries. The good social worker knows, particularly in a therapy setting, that those he or she helps will become dependent on him or her at some point. The social worker cannot encourage that dependence because true helping is allowing clients to help themselves. That is easier said than done. Sometimes you could be tempted to let a client hang onto your coattails because it feels good to be needed and admired. You have to be able to let go of your clients when they are ready to go.

You must also be able to stay separate from the client's problems, or you will find yourself sinking into them. When you work with a client, you cannot confuse the situation by playing racquetball with him or her after sessions. You should not enter into deals with clients, and you do not date them, no matter how attractive they are or how close they may be to terminating services. When you enter into an arrangement to help someone, you make an unwritten deal to focus on his or her problems. You owe it to the client to leave your own troubles and expectations out of it. If you tend to feel depressed because you overidentify with your clients and their problems, it will take a lot of energy to maintain your boundaries in this work. Having a strong sense of self helps to avoid losing yourself in other people's problems.

Whatever your particular prejudices are, if you cannot keep them out of your encounters with clients, you will not be helping them. That is not to say that you must not have any convictions. It merely means that you should not push your values on the client. Judging someone harshly only alienates both of you. If you categorize people before getting to know them, you are too judgmental to be working with them in this fashion. You support people by valuing their humanity, not by whether they live up to your expectations.

On the subject of listening, the good social worker listens with heart as well as ears. To treat a client with respect, you have to value what he or she says and how he or she defines the problem. You cannot listen to a few words and then take over the story. You keep listening until he or she has finished talking, and even then you try to hear what is not being said. A good listener is not quick to jump to conclusions.

Are you someone to whom other kids confide their problems? If so, it is probably because you are a good listener and can keep your mouth shut afterward. If you are not a good listener, it is another trait you can cultivate. Practice listening to others. Don't prepare your response while they are still talking. Having a ready reply makes it seem as though you had stopped listening halfway through their talking. Let them finish, and if necessary repeat the gist of what they said to be sure you understood it.

Are you good at keeping secrets? In social work there are always secrets to be kept. Confidentiality demands that you not discuss your caseload with others, that you not report names to other agencies (except in the case of abuse), and that you not joke about clients with others. (Good sense also dictates all the above). You can't titillate your roommate with, "Guess who came into the mental-health center today?" or "Guess how much the Thompsons make a year?" On the other hand, if you uncover a situation involving child abuse you are obligated by law to report it. Some secrets are not meant to be kept.

You need to empathize with the people you help. If you don't have empathy to begin with, you can't learn it in school; you can't order it from a catalog. Empathy is not the same as sympathy, which is misconstrued as pity. People in need do not want pity. Employees coming to you to settle a dispute do not want you to feel sorry for them. They want you to understand how the situation feels to them so that you can do something about it. Empathy is stepping into the other person's shoes for the moment. If you cannot imagine how it feels for a woman to have to send her children to bed hungry because she does not have enough money to buy food, you cannot help her. Empathy is understanding another person's predicament without condoning how she got into the predicament.

Of course, you must not go to the other extreme of getting so bogged down worrying about this mother that you can't sleep at night. You will not be helpful then, either, because you will be expending too much energy carrying *her* burdens. Empathy is the ability to see through another person's eyes; perspective allows you to step back and remember that you are not that person, but someone in a position to help him or her.

Successful social workers are assertive without being aggressive. If you are to advocate for other people, you have to stand up for them. That does not mean being haughty or demanding. It means standing up for what you believe even when it is scary to do so. Fortunately, even if you are shy, assertiveness is a trait you can learn. Often it comes from experience and self-confidence. Otherwise you can enroll in special assertiveness training groups.

To be an effective social worker you must have handled (or be handling) your personal problems. You cannot allow your own troubles to creep into sessions with clients. You cannot allow your problem with authority figures to affect your discussions with your boss. Social workers are human beings, and we all have our own idiosyncrasies and problems. We need to take care of our problems first, because people who come to us for help are looking for guidance in their own problems.

If you have read this far you may have noticed that I have not mentioned that you need to be an honor-roll student to be a social worker. Not all intelligent people get good grades. Some have a sixth sense about people and the way to help them. You don't get grades for intuition. Besides, you can always improve your grades, but you cannot readily develop that knack for understanding people. Sensitivity and common sense are far more valuable than book knowledge. (Nonetheless, I will show you ways to make the best of your high school years if getting good grades is a problem for you. You do have to get into college to specialize in social work.)

If you are not at the top of your class academically, it's still okay. You will have to read a lot, however, because effective social workers must keep abreast of current theories and research findings in their area of specialization. If you are not an avid reader, cultivate the habit now.

Notice, too, that I have not said your odds of getting a job are enhanced by being a male or a female. The sad thing is that the lower-paying social work positions are usually occupied by women. The more prestigious, higher-paying positions are often held by men, or evenly divided with women. Women first dominated the profession because it was considered by many to be a supplementary form of income. Women whose husbands had high-paying jobs could live comfortably on a social worker's salary; men who were a family's sole source of support could not.

If money is your greatest concern, this is probably not the field for you. You can make a good living as a social worker, but you would have to enter the private sector for a larger salary.

If you have all or most of the above qualities, you still may not be right for people-oriented jobs. For example, you would not do well in employment-counseling jobs in which you earn a commission by matching clients with jobs. If you have the "social worker" mentality, you could become overinvolved with the clients.

A similar problem happens in sales. As a salesman, your objective is to sell as much as possible. If you are sidetracked by people's problems, you do not make the necessary sales. If you're more concerned with "bettering mankind" you will not necessarily be a good salesman.

Human resource departments in major businesses formerly used social workers to mediate disputes.

Nowadays they are seeking people who have specific degrees in Human Resources. Companies have found that social workers cannot always separate the work-related problem from the client's other problems. What starts out as a request to aid management turns into an ongoing session with the employee. "Social workers get too involved," these companies say.

Problems exist in social work as in every other profession and are explained in detail in Part II. The greatest danger in the helping professions—whether it be psychology or social work—is *burnout*. It is hard to give of yourself every day and get little back. Generally, social work is not a profession in which you can see instant results from your work. When someone breaks a leg, the doctor sets the bone. When the bone has healed, the cast comes off and the doctor knows he has done his job. It is not so simple for the social worker. In Human Services you may initially help a family get welfare assistance, but their problems have not ended. Follow-ups and more help are usually needed. Therapy clients are not necessarily "cured" in one session. In fact, you will not necessarily "cure" them in any number of sessions. All this repetitive work, coupled with low pay, can lead to burnout.

Burnout happens in all professions, but it can happen quicker in social work if you are expecting to see instant results for your efforts. Or if you're expecting any special notice or reward. Social work efforts are not always appreciated initially, and it is frustrating to think you do not make a difference. That is why social workers should make the most of their off-duty and vacation time. Engage in hobbies and activities that are rewarding in themselves.

When you're burned out, you don't want to go to work. You're tired and can't think creatively. Talking about it with colleagues or supervisors can help.

But by the same token, words cannot convey the satisfaction of having successfully intervened in someone's life. It is a good feeling to know that you *have* made a difference. And although the work can be grueling, it is rarely dull, because people are rarely dull.

4

Educational Preparation

This chapter discusses the best way to prepare for the social work profession. First, let's discuss the several social work degrees, the merits of each, and the drawbacks of degrees in a related field.

Many people get their first job when they have completed their BSW (Bachelor of Social Work) degree. Not all colleges offer this degree, however, so check into the program's availability when you select your college. With a BSW you can enter some social work jobs, but nowadays employers are demanding the MSW (Master of Social Work) as a prerequisite.

The BSW is granted after completion of four years of college and the required number of hours specializing in social work. Even at the undergraduate level, you are expected to complete a field placement working as a social worker intern in a community agency, supervised by both your social work instructor and a supervisor in the agency. Nonetheless, the jobs you can pursue with only a BSW are limited. To be a therapist (a clinical social worker) or to work in a business setting, you need an MSW. This degree is a two-year, six-credit-hour program beyond the bachelor's degree. Although MSW programs vary in curricula, as a rule you will be required to take courses in five areas: theories of human behavior, social policy, research, social work practice, and a practicum. During the first year you will spend a couple of days a week working at an agency (or with some other social work group) to integrate what you are learning with what goes on in the real world. In the second year the last semester may be devoted entirely to your field placement, or practicum. Between the first and second year of coursework you may be required to pass an examination. Failure may preclude you from continuing until you pass the section of the test you failed.

The cost of the MSW program varies greatly from university to university, state to state. My sources tell me they've paid $15,000 while others have paid $50,000 to obtain their degree. Fortunately, grants, scholarships, and student loans are available to help with the cost. Instructors will advise you of pertinent grant money, but you'd also be wise to check with the financial aid office of each school.

Beyond the MSW and BSW are the DSW (Doctor of Social Work) and the PhD in Social Work. With the current emphasis on specialization and longer years of schooling, these degrees may become more popular. At the moment, however, doctoral degrees are needed more for teaching than anything else.

Schools are now offering other social work degrees, such as the Bachelor of Arts in Social Work and the Master of Arts in Social Work. These degrees should not differ in course emphasis, but employers who are used to the BSW and MSW may not give the same status to the holders of these other degrees. You will need to check in your state whether the BAs and MAs are considered the equivalent of the BSW and MSW degrees.

If you are serious about going into social work, go as far in your education as you can afford. When I returned to graduate school, I couldn't decide between two master's programs—one in the Psychology department (Human Relations) and the other specifically in

Social Work. Since my goal was to work as a Psychiatric Social Worker, I assumed either degree would be applicable. I finally chose the Human Relations degree for practical reasons: I could work on it at night while holding down a job during the day. With the social work program, I would have to take classes and do field placement during the day. To manage, I would have to change to a night job, and I didn't think I could handle that and school too.

Trying to make the best of both worlds, I took social work classes in addition to my Human Relations work, but I specialized in marriage and family counseling within my own program. Now, you would have thought that in the long run I was better prepared to go into counseling than someone who had not had courses in counseling and theory. I learned—too late—that the social work profession was beginning to recognize only those who had specialized in that program. I could do the work—counseling families—but I was not eligible to call myself a social worker; I was a social work assistant.

In the future, if the NASW is successful, only those with a specific degree in social work will be able to hold down traditional social work jobs. By the time you finish college, social work assistants will probably be a thing of the past. Social work professors and members of the NASW believe (and I do not dispute it) that only those who have been steeped in the social work philosophy, theory, and systems approach can perform as social workers. People with a background in Sociology, Psychology, or Education have a different theoretical frame of reference. Although they may be excellent clinicians because of their experience, they will not be admitted to the fold.

There is no point in arguing the merits of this decision. What is important for you to know is that a Master's degree in Sociology or Social Science is not the same as a social work degree. To qualify for certain social work positions, particularly the higher-paying ones, you need the MSW.

How do you find the right program? We've included a list at the back of this book of all the schools in the United States offering the MSW degree.

Some 400 undergraduate programs in social work and 100 graduate programs are available.

It is an easy matter to narrow down your college choices to a geographical area and then look through the catalogs for colleges that offer the BSW and MSW. If you live in an area where a degree program in social work is not offered, consider an extension program. Many colleges offer extension courses in social work in a locale away from their campus. You can do the first year wherever the courses are given close by, but you will have to commute to the college campus for your second year. The commuting may not be so bad, however; it may amount only to one day a week of classes. The rest of the time, you will probably do a field placement—a job—and that can be right in your hometown as long as you have an MSW supervisor to oversee your work.

How you finance your college degree may be another sticking point. All colleges and universities have financial aid offices, and people there can help you apply for guaranteed loans and scholarships.

By the time you are looking toward your MSW you'll be at least twenty-two years old, since you will have completed a four-year college course first. For many students those next two years may seem impossible. How can you pay for your schooling even if you do land a scholarship? There is still rent to pay and groceries to buy.

Talking to the financial aid office people may give you some ideas. Some students leave school temporarily to work for an agency that agrees to finance their schooling after roughly five years of work. They agree to repay the agency with two more years of work, and they receive not only their schooling and books, but also a stipend to live on while in school. Other students take advanced placement classes so they can continue in their present job. The second year of the MSW is required on-campus work, so they have to finish their schooling in the regular program, but many find a paying practicum.

Your guidance counselor can be of immeasurable assistance in finding a school that suits you. He or she can also help you figure out how you and your family can pay for your education.

How should you go about choosing a college? You should be thinking about your college choice when you are a junior in high school, not two weeks before graduation. You need time for you and your parents to visit the campuses, talk to the deans, and get an overall feel for the college. In your junior year, start consulting college catalogs: you can either borrow them from the guidance office or write to the colleges for them. Consider these variables: how far away the schools are, how much they cost, what courses they offer, and what type of students they attract.

GEOGRAPHY

Consider how close to your family you want to be in the next four years. If you choose a college on the other side of the country, you may be stranded for several months at a stretch. On the other hand, if you choose a school twenty miles up the road, consider whether or not you have really left home.

Consider, too, the environment of the schools. Are they located in the big city, the mountains, or near other schools? If you are a skier, it might be fun to go to a college in the mountains where you can spend your weekends skiing. On the other hand, if you select a college for its party atmosphere you may not get much of an education in the long run. Geography is important; it will help to pare down the number of possible choices.

COSTS

When I selected my undergraduate college I never considered the cost. I simply assumed that my father would pay for it, which he did—for the next ten years. It didn't occur to me until later that he was also paying for my older brother to go to college at the same time. When all is said and done and you're working, it probably won't matter that you went to a New England college that cost $26,000 a year. If you choose a college that costs more than you or your parents can easily afford, you won't enjoy the experience because you'll have to worry each semester whether the money is there for you to continue.

COURSES OFFERED

Obviously, it makes no sense to pick a college without checking to see if it offers the degree you want. Courses in social work or elementary education may not be available at a liberal arts college. You may have to go on to graduate school before you can get a good job.

Next, consider the size of the classes. Will you be in lecture room-size classes of 100-plus students, or will you have classes of ten to fifteen students? Does that matter? Do you want teacher/student interaction or greater anonymity? Catalogs do not specify the size of classes, but they no doubt are related to the size of the college or university. Ask about it in your interview.

ATMOSPHERE

You are going to spend four years at this school, so be sure to select one where you'll be comfortable. Notice the students when you visit the campuses. Are they relaxed? Decked out in formal attire? Which appeals to you? What is the atmosphere in the library? Where do the students study? What about extracurricular events? What kinds of sports are played? Is there much school spirit, and does that even matter to you?

Consider the academic standards of the school. If you would have a tough time maintaining a good grade point average, it may not be the school for you. You need to get into graduate school, and a poor showing during your undergraduate years will not help you. Most graduate schools expect you to take a graduate record examination (GRE) to be admitted to a program, but if your grade point average is high enough they will rely on your academic record alone.

Speaking of exams, you will probably have to take college entrance exams—either the SAT or ACT—as part of the college application process. If you are not a good test-taker (and not everyone is), consider which schools rely least on the exam scores. Some colleges have a "cut-off point," and anyone presenting scores below that point is not accepted. In the end, your test scores may limit your choices.

When you have narrowed down your choices to a few colleges, visit them and arrange for interviews. If the school is not sure about your academic qualifications, a good interview may tip the scales in your favor. When you visit the campus, seek out students in the library or student union and ask them what they like about the school. Most students like to talk about their school—the bad points as well as the good. Listen to them on both counts.

In the end, you will have to set priorities; it's a rare school that will meet all your expectations. Decide what is most important to you—how close you'll be to home, how much the school costs, or whether you'll get to go skiing on weekends.

Once you have decided on a school and decided on a major—in this case, social work—you still have plenty of leeway with other courses. Aside from a few "fun" courses, you might consider a business course or two and some anthropology courses. The business courses will help if that is the branch of social work you eventually choose, and the anthropology courses will help to give you an overall appreciation of other cultures.

When you're considering a graduate program in social work, look over the specific courses available at several of the colleges that offer the MSW degree. Not all graduate programs are alike. This is important to remember if you're interested in doing clinical work (providing therapy to clients). Before you can be board certified (and we talk about board certification in the next chapter), you have to qualify to take the exam. Only those students who have accumulated enough hours of clinical coursework (for example, psychopathology courses) will qualify to take the exam. Many MSW programs do not offer sufficient clinical courses to prepare you for board certification. If you have any questions about the suitability of your school's program, ask whether its graduates are eligible to take the exam for board certification. If you're not satisfied with the answer, write for more information to:

The American Board of Examiners in Clinical
Social Work (ABE)
Three Mill Road
Suite 306
Wilmington, Delaware 19806
or call: (302) 425-5730

What else can you do in college to give you a head start in social work? Many agencies offer summer intern programs that can give you an idea of the jobs available once you're out in the real world. You will be paid for these internships and can learn at the same time. The contacts you make will be invaluable too. Sometime soon you'll be looking for work. It's nice to have someone who remembers your work or who will be a reference for you.

But perhaps we have jumped too far ahead. Right now—even in high school—there are things you can do to prepare for social work. Volunteer jobs are a good place to start; you'll get a feel for the work and you'll be needed. You can volunteer in nursing homes, in hospitals, or in day-care or senior citizen agencies. It's better to find out now if you enjoy working with people in this fashion than to spend a fortune on education first. Furthermore, volunteer work will give you a head start in the job search later on, because you'll be a known quantity with work experience and references.

What if you are not a particularly good student? Can you still get into college? You will have an opportunity to shine in the interview or in the admission application essay. If your grades were poor in your early years of high school but improved in your later years, you can show that you take your studies more seriously now.

But what can you do right now? You may not have developed good study habits. Organizing your time so that you study more efficiently is the key to better grades. With homework assignments, be sure you know exactly what the teacher wants. Check it out if you're not certain. Tackle your assignments when your energy is up—not at 10 PM the night before they're due. If you have a lot of homework, break it up into manageable blocks. Do some subjects before dinner and the others afterward. Reward yourself for completing assignments; take frequent short breaks, but don't get sidetracked watching television. Make it a habit to do assignments when they are due. Some students make the mistake of reading the whole book when only a few chapters are assigned. Then they have no time for their other work. Do what you can with the time you've got. Organizing your time simply means establishing priorities. Do the important things first, then move on to those "other" things you enjoy. Always have something fun to do after schoolwork, especially if you consider it boring or hard. Otherwise, you'll come to resent your homework and eventually find excuses not to do it.

Since social work is a profession of interaction, it is useful to join groups like the Drama Club, sports teams, or 4-H Club. Groups give you a sense of camaraderie and an outlet for your energy. There are all kinds of ways to "be with people." Just having fun is valid too. You have plenty of time ahead to get serious with your life's work.

Professional Organizations and Licensure

The most important organization to join if you are a social worker or a social work student is the National Association of Social Workers (NASW). It is expensive (around $150 for professionals, much less for students); but it is enormously helpful, and it lends credibility to your name. The NASW publishes a journal and newsletters. You can also purchase liability and life insurance at reduced cost through this group.

You can order *Social Work*, the NASW journal, which costs $67 a year for nonmembers but is free with membership. It publishes scholarly articles on social work policy, theory, and practice. The advertisements alone are instructive; you can find out about workshops and new books. The newsletter carries information on job opportunities around the country, area workshops, and conferences.

Membership in NASW gives you two kinds of support. First, it is a nationwide lobbying organization for passage of laws pertinent to social workers. You can express your opinions on such bills and be assured that social workers' best interests will be represented. As a member you also indicate to others that you are a professional, that you belong to a group larger than yourself, and that you adhere to certain standards of professional behavior.

Second, you can attend meetings of your local chapter. Connecting with other social workers for camaraderie and an exchange of ideas is called networking. These people can share job opportunities with you as they crop up.

NASW is an important professional group for social workers. The dues, while hefty to those in lower-paying jobs, are sometimes covered by agencies whose employers require you to join.

Why should social work students want to join NASW? Mostly for the networking opportunities and the information contained in the newsletter and journal. For a nominal fee, student members can participate in their local chapter and get a firsthand look at the social worker experience.

NASW currently boasts 155,000 members and fifty-five chapters nationwide. For more information on membership, you may call 1 (800) 742-4089 or write to:

NASW
750 First Street, NE
Suite 700
Washington, DC 20002-4241

When you move to another state, transferring your membership to another NASW chapter will help you fit into the new social work community.

Another professional organization is the Academy of Certified Social Workers. Members are entitled to use the initials ACSW after their name. As a professional, you will have to decide whether membership is worth the expense (approximately $50 a year) and passing the required exam. For many people, it is unnecessary; others want the prestige it carries, indicating that they possess the knowledge and professional experience to have won membership.

For those of you going into clinical practice, you may want to become board certified. National board certification has been available since 1987. Earning the right to put BCD (Board Certified Diplomate in Clinical Social Work) after your name is worth every penny of the $250 it costs to take the exam. National board certification for clinical social workers is conducted by the American Board of Examiners in Clinical Social Work (ABC). Board certification for social workers is similar to board certification for doctors. It tells your clients that you've spent many hours in clinical work, and that you were sufficiently knowledgeable to pass a rigorous national exam.

In order to qualify for this exam, you must have worked as a social worker for five years (after obtaining your MSW), with 3,000 of the required 7,500 clinical hours supervised by a licensed social worker. You must have completed an MSW program that focused on clinical knowledge and skills and is accredited by the Council on Social Work Education. You must possess the highest licensure possible for your state. The exam is reportedly very difficult. Once you have passed the exam, your board certification is valid for whatever state in which you happen to be practicing. For example, if you are board certified while living in Oklahoma, you need not take another exam to be board certified if you move to Texas. Licensing requirements vary from state to state, but board certification is national. You will never have to take another board certification exam once you've passed the first one. You will need twenty hours a year of continuing education credits, however, to maintain board certification.

Another aspect of the professional organizations is that they benefit the public as well as the social worker. If an NASW member behaves inappropriately with a client, the group has the power to censure his or her actions. It can do that by canceling membership or openly admonishing the member, depending on the seriousness of the misbehavior. By belonging to the NASW or ACSW, you agree to abide by a professional code of ethics. If you fail to abide by those standards, you forfeit your right to membership.

Other professional organizations and journals are discussed in the chapters on the various fields of social work in Part II of this book.

Other powerful organizations for social workers to join are the hospital unions, which represent the employees' interests in exchange for membership and dues. The dues are relatively small in comparison to the benefits. Don't underestimate the power of a union—even a small one.

Licensure varies from state to state, and you cannot practice social work (and be reimbursed by insurance companies) without it. The reasons for licensure are clear: It certifies that you are qualified for the job, and it gives the licensing board a means of discipline should you betray its standards. It also serves to protect the public from fraudulent and abusive practices.

To obtain a license a social worker must have graduated from an accredited school. To receive the title of Social Worker, he or she must possess the MSW degree. Following graduation, the person must work for two years as a social worker under supervision of a licensed MSW. During that time the person is considered "license-eligible"; many agencies can hire him or her even though the services are not yet reimbursable by insurance companies. This is mostly an issue for clinical social workers who work in an outpatient facility or in private practice, because agencies lose money if they cannot collect reimbursement on unlicensed personnel.

There are at least two national social work exams, and the states specify which one they expect you to pass. If you are a good test-taker and know your field, you should have no difficulty with the exam. It is hard, and the questions are tricky, but after two years of post-graduate work and two years of experience you should be able to answer them. When you apply to take the exam, you indicate an area of specialization in which you will additionally be tested. The choices are clinical social work practice, social work administration, and social work planning and community organization.

The usual license fee is $50. The fee for the licensing exam is an additional $90 to $120. If you fail the exam the first time it costs an additional $90 to $120 to have a second shot.

When you have passed the exam you receive your numbered license and details of all the codes of behavior and rules to which you must subscribe

Your license is your key to a host of social work positions, so maintain it whether you stay in practice or not. Maintaining your license means renewing it yearly or every other year when it comes up for renewal, and paying the fee.

In addition to the fee for license renewal you have to present credit hours of continuing education in social work—classroom study, workshops, or correspondence courses. Usually the number of hours is twelve. The reason for this requirement should be obvious; you need to keep abreast of current theories and research findings to perform an adequate job. Nobody ever stops learning.

Before you wrinkle your nose in disgust, let me assure you that acquiring continuing education credits is not such a bad thing. Workshops, which your agency will probably pay for you to attend, are given in all parts of the country.

As I said earlier, licensure varies from state to state. States may not transfer licensure from another state without requiring the applicant to pass his or her exam.

You should keep up your social work license even if you are not practicing. It is a small matter to pay the renewal fee, and it's often fun to participate in workshops for continuing education credits. Letting your license lapse, however, and then deciding to get back into social work may mean facing the licensing exam all over again, which is costly and a hassle. If there is any chance you might return to the profession, you should hang on to your license.

By the way, you can be licensed without an MSW, but a BSW is the very minimum. In that case your license might read: Licensed Social Work Associate instead of Licensed Social Worker, but it is the magic word licensed that matters. Go ahead and display your license on the wall of your office; you've earned it. Being licensed says that you are credible and accountable—and worthy of hiring. If you are board certified, too, make sure that information finds its way into every résumé you send out. It says: You're worth it!

PART II

A CLOSER LOOK AT SOCIAL WORK

Medical Social Worker

Salary range: $23,000 to $40,000 (the higher salaries reflect supervisory responsibilities).

JOB DESCRIPTION

A medical social worker works in a hospital and can be assigned to cover any number of wards. If you think of this person as a combination finder-of-resources and crisis worker, you have a good idea of what he or she does. When a patient is admitted, any number of people might decide that he needs to talk with the social worker as well as see the doctor. Let me give you an example. Suppose a thirteen-year-old girl is brought into the emergency room, barely alive from a suicidal drug overdose. Of course, the doctors and nurses do their best to resuscitate her and stabilize her condition, but then what? That is where the medical social worker comes in. It is his or her job to assess the girl's drug habit and to arrange a meeting with her family so they can decide where she should get help for her underlying problem. A medical hospital can take care of the patient's physical needs, but it cannot prolong her stay just because the doctors don't know what else to do. It is the social worker's job to locate a drug program or psychiatric counseling for the girl and help her schedule an appointment. If the girl remains suicidal, the social worker will consider psychiatric hospitalization and recommend that to the girl, her family, and the doctors. As you can see, a medical social worker has to be able to intervene quickly and appropriately in a crisis.

Some patients who are hospitalized because of a stroke or a heart attack need help when they are discharged. Families may not know whom to contact for assistance. The medical social worker knows the resources available in the community and can make the initial call to an inhome nursing service. The social worker can also meet with the family to discuss the patient's condition and offer emotional support and reassurance.

As you can imagine, the medical social worker's day is never the same, especially if he or she works in the emergency room. In that area one cannot anticipate what services will be needed because the types of patients change from day to day.

If you are good at thinking on your feet, if you are sensitive and caring and not afraid of the emotional difficulty you will encounter, you would do well here. Naturally, in a hospital you have to face painful situations and, on occasion, death. Not everyone gets well. As a medical social worker, you cannot afford to become too involved with the patients because you can lose your objectivity. You are with them only a short time before you turn them over to other services.

As a supervisor in the social work department, you do everything just mentioned, plus oversee your department (which means making certain that the other social workers are doing their jobs), prepare and manage a budget (because you must decide how much you need for expenses: salaries, workshop and conference money for your staff, and an indigent fund for needy patients), and represent the hospital at community functions. Supervisors are paid well, and they earn every penny.

The medical social worker does not have to see everyone who is admitted to the hospital. Sometimes a doctor suggests seeing one of his patients; sometimes the nurses spot a patient who is depressed or needs "something extra." Social workers themselves routinely go over the list of new patients and those to be discharged, so that they have an idea who might need their services. "So George Henley is being discharged on Thursday. Does his family know the date for the Head Injury Group meeting?" That sort of thing.

Even the patient can ask to see a social worker. The medical social worker may need to do some individual counseling before referral to an outpatient therapist. Counseling can include crisis-intervention work, which helps victims of child abuse, sexual abuse, or marital problems, and supportive work, when someone has just been told he has a life-threatening illness.

ETHICAL DILEMMAS

As our medical technology increases, doctors are able to extend people's lives, sometimes beyond the point at which they can be enjoyed. How do quality-of-life issues affect the medical social worker?

It is the medical social worker's job not only to help the patient cope, but also to help the family and friends who support him. If a patient is no longer able to decide for himself whether or not to continue receiving treatment the family must make that decision for him. Doctors are understandably reluctant to make the decision alone. It may fall to you, then, to assist the family in its decision-making. It won't be your sole decision, but you can provide support to those people who are struggling with the task. Better to explore your thoughts and feelings well before you attempt to work with others.

Consider these questions. Is it ever morally right to terminate medical treatment? If doctors have the skills to keep people alive, must they use them in every case, even if the treatment is only prolonging the patient's suffering?

If a baby is born with multiple problems, like respiratory failure, severe brain damage, or heart defects, should the family urge the doctors to do everything possible to keep her alive?

When resources are limited, how do you support families who are told that their loved one does not qualify for treatment?

What do you do if you're working with a patient who refuses to follow your advice? A competent person has the right to refuse treatment, even if that refusal may result in death.

Where will you release the elderly man who wants to go home, but you know won't take his medicine correctly? Should you send him to a nursing home, even though he says he'd rather fend for himself?

These are some of the ethical dilemmas you'll face, now that modern medicine has prolonged life.

The Good Points

If you like working with people and if you have a good idea of community resources (or how to find them), you will like the variety of experiences encountered in this job. One social worker says that the reason she likes her job so much is because it's never the same two days in a row.

As in most career fields, it is nice to feel needed, and nowhere is that so readily apparent as in this field. You are able to provide a tangible service, whether that be arranging an appointment for someone to see another therapist or finding financial assistance for someone who doesn't realize that any exists for him. In medical social work you see immediate results because you work with the patient only while he is in the hospital. You make the connection for him, and you sit and listen until it is time for him to go. When your service is appreciated, it is hard not to like your job.

As a medical social worker, you work with excellent medical professionals—doctors, nurses, physical therapists. Working around people who are knowledgeable and caring enhances your own experience with the patient.

THE DISADVANTAGES

Depending on your point of view, the above list of good points can be turned around and considered disadvantages. You may not like having your day unstructured—or structured according to everyone else's needs. You may not like running around playing "catch up" with patients who seem to have more needs than you have time for in a day.

Another disadvantage might be not getting to form long-term relationships with patients. Your job is to assist the patient while he is there and refer him to someone else upon discharge. Sometimes it is hard to break attachments you have formed, particularly with children.

Working with a variety of personnel means that you will have your share of "difficult" colleagues. They will not all be talented and helpful. Since your job is to interact with the doctors and nurses, it makes for a delicate situation when you have to work with someone you do not like or respect. As a social worker, it is not your job to side with a patient against a doctor.

Most people find it hard to work with families whose loved ones are dying, particularly if they are children. It takes a special kind of person to do so on a regular basis, so unless you volunteer for the assignment you probably won't encounter it routinely. Nonetheless, you must accept that some of those you try to help will not get better, no matter how hard you will them to live. You cannot take this job home with you, so you must learn early to separate their pain from yours. Again, much easier said than done.

DEGREE REQUIREMENTS
Because this job requires a broad knowledge of social services in the community and the ability to assess and intervene in medical situations, specialization in social work is expected. Most hospitals require the MSW, because nowadays more social workers have the degree and therefore the hospital can use them. You may also want a license in clinical social work practice or administration, depending on your role.

Some hospitals have used social workers with only a BSW, but most refuse to accept a person with a non-social work degree, even from a related field.

In this position you need the advanced degree and serveral years of experience for consideration in the larger hospitals.

OPPORTUNITIES IN THE FIELD
States vary in needs and pay scales. Some large city hospitals may be saturated with medical social workers, whereas rural hospitals may be in great need of even one BSW.

As a rule, however, medical social workers are in high demand. The job tends to have more women than men, although in the supervisory roles you may find a higher percentage of men.

OPPORTUNITY FOR ADVANCEMENT
Opportunity for advancement means the opportunity to grow into other jobs in the hospital that either require more skills or demand more of your time. As a medical social worker, your job is on par with other social workers. The only upward move would be to the

head of your department, and that slot is unlikely to open up until the department head leaves. Because hospital social work departments tend to be small, you probably have little chance of immediate advancement.

Sometimes opportunities for advancement exist in another hospital. When you have established yourself in the field and accumulated some years of experience, you are marketable anywhere.

Opportunities to make more money elsewhere will always present themselves. You then have to decide what compromises you want to make for them. My friend had the opportunity to leave her part-time position in one hospital to take a supervisor's role at another hospital closer to home. She stood to make more money in the new job, and she could walk to work. However, the supervisor's position was full time, so she would have to forfeit some time with her family for the increased benefits and responsibilities.

How to Break into the Job

Medical social workers cannot just walk into a hospital and offer their MSW in exchange for a job. Employers are looking for social workers who have experience in hospital settings or similar agencies. The social workers have to know the resources in the community and possess the skill to work with terminally ill patients, irate families, and suicidal clients. Obviously, the social worker fresh out of college is not a good candidate. In my experience in psychiatric work, the more experienced social worker tends to be the most unflappable. You need to be calm and collected when faced with an emergency or when you run out of resources. Patience and an awareness of the limits to your "giving" will come later in your career. Hospital administrators know that.

If you are interested in medical social work you should begin early to learn as much as you can about hospitals. Volunteer to be a candy striper, or sign on during the summer as a nurse's aide. The candidate who already has an understanding of the inner workings of a hospital is that much further ahead in finding future employment.

If possible, select a field placement in a hospital while you are in college. Do an independent study project interviewing a medical social worker to learn firsthand about the job—and for later reference when you are looking for employment.

When you have graduated and received your MSW, apply for a job even if none is currently available. Positions come and go, sometimes rapidly, so it pays to get your name in, and check periodically to see where you stand on the list.

In the meantime, take a social work job in a community agency—if nothing else to your liking comes along—so that you can familiarize yourself with the resources available in your community. Keep a file of names of agencies and their services or of helpful people you have met. You never know when you may need their help again.

Stay involved by making yourself known in the community. That does not mean volunteering for every job that comes along in your NASW group, nor does it mean making a nuisance of yourself. It simply means making yourself visible in a professional way. Keep the network open and you will hear when there is a job opening in your field. And when one comes your way, look back over all your experience (the volunteer work, the community service, the practicums you have held) and put yourself forward in the best possible light.

HELPFUL HINTS ON THE JOB

1. Familiarize yourself with the *PDR* (*Physicians' Desk Reference*) so that you know about

medications your patients are using and their side effects.

2. Read health-related journals. A good one to subscribe to is *Health and Social Welfare,* which can be ordered through NASW, 7981 Eastern Avenue, Silver Spring, MD 20910.

3. Keep adding to that file and periodically check it over. Reestablish contact with people who have previously helped you.

4. Maintain a good relationship with your community sources, including the mental-health center. You never know when you might need a favor fast.

5. Learn to organize your time right from the start.

7

School Social Worker

Salary range: $18,000 to $35,000 (depending on locale and size of school system).

JOB DESCRIPTION

A school social worker functions much like a clinical social worker, except that the clients are usually students. The teacher goes to school to teach her students, and the social worker goes there to help students handle their emotional problems. Naturally, the social worker does not know who will come through the door for help each day unless specific appointments are scheduled. The crises, of course, cannot be scheduled. The social worker meets with troubled students in a way that guidance counselors are not necessarily trained to do. Often the school social worker has been trained in clinical work (either in a psychiatric setting or in another counseling agency), so that he or she is prepared to deal with emotionally distraught persons.

What kind of problems does a school social worker encounter? As you can imagine, he or she will probably see students with noticeable behavioral problems. Not necessarily the student who acts up in class once, but the student who repeatedly gets into trouble from smart-mouthing the teacher or hurting students, including himself. The social worker can explore what is going on in the classroom as well as in the student's home to account for such hostility. What he discovers may lead him to suggest individual counseling with the student, family counseling if the student's parents and siblings seem to be part of the problems, or joint meetings with the student's teachers and principal.

Working with troubled students is not the whole job, however. Some school social workers routinely work with all the students in special education classes, assessing whether or not their needs are being met. The paperwork for these students turns into a mountain if you are not careful to write your notes promptly and succinctly.

The social worker also attends meetings regarding the students' academic or emotional needs, and even runs workshops with the students to build their self-esteem.

Some social workers handle three or four schools in a city, which does not give them much time to "fit in" anywhere.

School social workers who are assigned to cover an alternative class for the regular school system may find their job better defined. Students in an alternative class are there usually because they did not fit in with the other students or teachers in mainstream classes. They may be seen as troublemakers or underachievers, so the social worker can anticipate some difficulty maintaining the student's interest in school.

Let me tell you a few typical situations as a school counselor in an alternative class. My first crisis was a girl who overdosed on a tranquilizer. She wound up in a hospital where her stomach was pumped and was later transferred to a psychiatric hospital for treatment of depression. Although she was no longer in my hands, I maintained contact with her to let her know we had not forgotten her.

Another student cut her wrists after a fight with her boyfriend. She received sutures and a night in the hospital, but when she refused psychiatric treatment she was released. Getting her into the mental-health center took most of the next day; I not only had to reassure her family but also convince the girl that therapy was not the end of the world. Perhaps the hardest part was securing an appointment for her at the center when they were booked weeks in advance. In this case I realized my shortcomings as a school counselor: I could not be responsible for a suicidal student; she had to be referred to someone in a psychiatric facility.

Often I had to take a student aside and remind her how important it was to finish school and how close she was to finishing. Sometimes she would be upset over an assignment, sometimes angry over trouble at home. In some cases I had to calm the student down when she was too angry to attend class; in others I had to calm down a parent who was upset with the limitations of our program.

The school social worker does not always handle monumental problems. Sometimes by leaving the door open, he or she encourages students to wander in "just to talk." Students often came by to see me, saying, "I don't have a problem or anything. I just came by to talk."

"Well, have a seat," I'd say, and next thing I knew I was hearing about a boyfriend on drugs, or a mother with a drinking problem, or the student's difficulty finding a summer job.

The school social worker's job, then, much like any social worker's, is defined by the problems of the clientele. In this case, it's the school system. Sometimes the problems are big and seemingly unmanageable; sometimes finding resources in the community for the student and his family is all that is needed.

THE GOOD POINTS

If you like an unstructured day and the hustle and bustle of the school setting, you will like this job. Like medical social work, this work never gets boring because people are never boring. Your day is your own, which means that you get to decide, more or less, how many students you will see or when you will give your next workshop.

If you enjoy kids in the first place—and that is necessary for this position—you will enjoy your work. Helping children sort out their problems, whether you work in elementary school or the higher grade levels, can be gratifying. Kids can be so appreciative.

Creating workshops designed to help kids feel good about themselves can be fun too. Most students will respond to your efforts, and that's a nice feeling.

And, of course, you have your summers off. You may receive some of the teachers' benefits (if you negotiate for them), such as tuition for further education courses and workshops.

THE DISADVANTAGES

The bad parts of this job mostly have to do with the extra running around that may be required. You may find yourself without an office, particularly if you cover more than one school. There's little worse than feeling like an official without an official place.

If you have trouble structuring your day, you will be at a true disadvantage because you will not have a supervisor reminding you what you need to do. In fact, in most districts you will not have a social work supervisor; you will be accountable to the school.

Another disadvantage can be feeling that what you have to offer is not appreciated. If you cannot talk freely with the teachers or other staff members, you will feel powerless to effect change for the kids. If you do have that trouble, however, you can usually switch to a school system in which you are more comfortable.

You will not have the opportunity to socialize with

other social workers on the job because very likely you will be the only one. That can be lonely.

The paperwork seems to be a universal complaint, but every profession has mountains of it. You need to make peace with paperwork early in your career, or you'll suffocate under the pileup.

DEGREE REQUIREMENTS

Currently, the school system itself sets the degree requirements for the job. The larger school districts expect the MSW because the additional years of experience and study are to their benefit. Other schools employ BSWs or even people with a Master's in a related field as long as they can get state licensure in some capacity. The requirements for licensure are tightening, however, which in essence means that most school systems are moving in the direction of hiring only MSWs.

OPPORTUNITIES IN THE FIELD

There is certainly room for more school social workers, but not all school districts can afford to hire one. This field is increasing in importance, so perhaps in the future the demand will be greater.

Women dominate this field for two reasons. First, of course, more women hold the MSW degree. Second, it is a great job for a mother with young children. School social workers have the same vacations as the teachers, so women like the job because it allows them to be at home with their children.

OPPORTUNITIES FOR ADVANCEMENT

The job offers no real upward mobility unless you are assigned to a large school with a social work department. Only then can you aspire to head the department, take increased job responsibilities, and earn substantially more money. Otherwise you may have to look into school districts that pay better salaries, offer more incentives (for example, paying part of your tuition if you return to school yourself), or are more conveniently located.

HOW TO BREAK INTO THE JOB

This is another job in which you can increase your worth to potential employers by having a thorough knowledge of your environment. How do you learn about the schools? Volunteer or get hired as a teacher's aide or in the Head Start program in your community. During the summer, involve yourself in recreational programs, which will bring you into contact with students of all ages.

School districts want people who are supportive of schools and have a working knowledge of the classroom. Former teachers fit in well. Beyond that, candidates need excellent counseling skills to handle emergencies. A school social worker needs to know when to treat someone and when to back off and refer the client to someone with more specialized skills. Only the experienced person knows his or her own limitations.

While working on your social work degree, take some education courses, and perhaps spend your field placement or a longer practicum in a school setting.

Get some training in clinical practice (counseling). Familiarize yourself with community resources; you will sometimes need to refer to other agencies and people for assistance beyond what you can provide. Attend school board meetings; these are usually open to the public. The more contacts you make even before you apply for a job, the better. Contacts become resources and potential references; you can never have too many of either. When you think you have sufficient experience and are licensed or license-eligible, apply to as many schools as you can.

You can find out where the jobs are only if you keep your ears and eyes open and let people know you are looking. When I enrolled my oldest child in kindergarten several years ago, I spent some time chatting with one of the guidance counselors there. It happened that the school was looking for a social worker, and she encouraged me to apply for the job—even though I assured her that I was not in the market.

Another way to bring yourself to the attention of the schools is to volunteer to teach a course in the adult education department. You will get minimal pay for teaching these classes (which can include anything from basket-weaving or aerobics to art history), but the idea is to get your foot in the door and keep your name circulating in a positive manner. You want administrators who pick up your job application to say, "Her? Oh, I know who she is."

Helpful Hints on the Job
1. Keep on top of your paperwork.
2. Subscribe to educational journals (or read them in the school library) to keep up with what is going on in the classroom and in educational trends.
3. Maintain your contacts with other agencies and people in the community; you never know when you might need a favor.
4. Stay involved in some physical activity or sport—you'll feel better, and it's a good way to "ventilate."
5. Recognize your place in the system so that you don't find yourself split off from your teaching colleagues.

8

Community Organization and Administration

Salary range: As a community organizer supported by funding grants, you can name your salary (as long as it is in line with similar professionals). In administrative work the salary varies with the size of the agency and whether or not it is privately funded. A reasonable range is $35,000 to $60,000.

JOB DESCRIPTION

In this chapter we shall look at the variety of jobs available when you go into community organization or rise in the ranks in administrative work. First let's look at the job of the community organizer.

As the name implies, this social worker goes out into the community and "organizes" things. He or she is not the social reformer who goes around organizing protests. Instead, he or she seeks to define a service that is lacking in the community and demonstrates how to fill that need. Let me give you an example.

When a colleague was in his second year of graduate school he worked out of the Area-Wide Aging Agency. As part of his practicum, he developed a plan to address the needs of the elderly crime victim. First he researched the literature. Then he made his own survey of the types of crime committed and the sites of the crimes. When he had accumulated the data through police reports and crime statistics, he formulated a mission (purpose for his proposal), his goals and objectives, and what it would cost in funding.

In this case the mission was to find out what types of crime were commited against the elderly and how the police department could have responded better. One of the objectives was to educate the police department about the elderly victim's needs. A special police person trained to deal with victims could be sent to each reported case. At that time there were no policemen who knew how to link the elderly person with community resources in case of burglary, who could counsel the victim, or help him reapply for his social security card if it had been stolen.

Another objective was to educate senior citizens about crimes committed against them and at the same time advise them of the agencies that could respond to their needs. Educating the senior citizen contingent meant speaking to them where they congregated—at senior citizen dinners and recreational centers.

The community organizer, then, must *define a problem* in the community and write a proposal to address that need. The proposal outlines the objectives, how much the mission will cost, and a means of evaluating whether or not the objectives were met.

All kinds of community jobs can be funded through state and federal monies. You need to uncover a need, propose a way to address it, and, of course, know where the dollars are.

Some social workers have tackled community revitalization projects, finding ways to bring a neighborhood back to life and helping the residents achieve that goal. First, you have to have a plan and the money to see the plan through, and then you have to have the heart to put the words into action. The job calls for diligence and persistence in digging up facts to support your plans, creativity in finding resources, and initiative. To remain steadily employed, you either have to keep writing grant proposals or tap into an agency that will continue to fund you because they believe in what you're doing.

One woman I know wondered how libraries funded their expansion. She discovered that library boards of trustees were not particularly adept at organizing expansion. They could not agree on what part of the library to expand or on how to raise funds. Sometimes they had not even assessed the community's needs for library services.

This woman devised a plan to help library boards learn how to expand their services. She learned all she could on the subject, and through experience helping her own library grow she became a consultant on the subject. People paid to have her show them a way to assess their community's needs for library services and then to fit it into their budget. She had seen a need and met it, following certain established procedures: she defined a diagnostic tool (the informal survey) and matched needs with money available for improvements. Thereafter she showed how to apply for grants and offered fund-raising techniques. As a coordinator for library renewal projects, she created her own consulting position.

If you choose to tackle this social work position, remember that you must know where the funding money is and be adept at writing grants to get it. You have to be a good salesman too; excellent persuasive skills are necessary for this job.

What about administrative work connected to community organization? In the recent past, it has been discovered that when a group of people get together to do something, the social worker among them usually takes over the leadership role. He or she possesses the skills to organize and supervise. In community projects social workers are willingly made project leaders—and hence, administrators.

Social workers have had much success running programs and even whole agencies. In Norman, Oklahoma, two huge agencies stand side by side. A female social worker (the first in the agency's forty-three-year history) is the deputy director of one agency. She is responsible for supervision of the staff, social services, medical records, and the psychology department, as well as being the school administrator. Next door at the mental-health center, another social worker is co-deputy director, responsible for supervising and staffing the whole facility and managing relations between the legislature, the Central Office, and the mental-health center. These two social workers head not only their departments but the agencies themselves.

Another colleague does a different kind of administrative job. He works as an auditor for the state, checking the various mental-health agencies for compliance with state statutes. His work takes him across the state auditing the agencies' records. This job requires that the social worker has a thorough knowledge of medical records and the diplomatic skills to urge compliance in recordkeeping.

Another colleague is the director of outpatient services in a large psychiatric hospital. He has authority over several programs: the outpatient programs, transitional living, and partial hospitalization. It is his job to staff and supervise these programs and to coordinate them with the other services of the hospital. It is also his job to promote these programs in the community by attending mental-health meetings and conferences throughout the state and the country. An administrator is responsible for everything that goes right (and wrong) in his or her programs, which means being aware of everything that goes on. He or she also has to project a positive image of the organization in the community, so part of the job is "politicking" with important people. An equally important task is educating the general public about the organization's services. The good administrator is not only a good administrator but also a practiced speaker and an engaging personality.

Since one of the authors is now in an administrative role at his agency, we have more insight into the good points and the disadvantages of this particular job.

THE GOOD POINTS

With any one of these jobs you will be attracted to the diversity of tasks. You do not do the same thing every day, even if you have the same responsibilities. You decide what needs to be done, and how. You have fewer people to answer to, although of course you have to be even more responsive to public opinion.

If you like responsibility, you will have plenty in the position. As a community organizer you are fully responsible for defining and funding your project. As an administrator you are someone else's boss and, as such, able to call some of your own shots. (Of course, there is a down side to increased responsibility.)

You will also like the independence this job offers; you create your own schedule and make your own decisions.

Real incentives to this job are the salary and prestige that come from running an organization. For some people there is satisfaction in running their own show, as the community organizer does. He or she meets interesting people and works with them on a collegial basis to influence change in the community.

Administrators enjoy more status and power. They are more involved in the decision-making of the agency or program and so have more direct input. In many cases, you have the opportunity to market yourself and your agency through radio and TV appearances (although some might consider this a disadvantage as much as an advantage.) You are given opportunities to make presentations and to involve yourself in more community activities. It helps to have a sense of humor.

There is the satisfaction of having created a program to meet the needs of a segment of the community. When you have done a job well and it is appreciated, you realize why you are in this line of work.

Lastly, you have the opportunity in some of these positions to travel to major cities in the line of duty—which is not to say that you can't make a vacation out of some of the better places. Administration isn't all work.

The Disadvantages

Most of the advantages just mentioned can be disadvantages to some people. Maybe you don't like added responsibility. Maybe you don't like feeling ultimately responsible for anything that goes wrong in the department. With increased responsibilities come increased hours too. Longer hours, a more serious attitude, and a greater distance to "fall from grace" make this a potentially exhausting job. You need a good deal of energy.

As an administrator, you are required to hire (and fire) your employees. You evaluate their performance and adherence to agency policy; if things are not going well, you let them know. If you have been promoted to administration from within your organization, you soon realize that you are no longer treated as a peer by those you now supervise. It may be confusing for all of you at first to get used to your administrative role.

As an administrator, you have two sets of people to account to: your supervisors (who have less of a personal interest in your staff) and your employees (who look to you to speak on their behalf). It takes an individual with good negotiating skills and infinite patience to handle this job.

Another disadvantage is that there is never enough time to get everything done—plan ahead, work on budgets, attend endless meetings, and stay abreast of current office situations.

Then, of course, there are office politics. You not only have to appease the people in your organization, but also the important people in the community who support you. You have to be careful not to step on people's toes. You may be expected to work with legislators on issues that directly affect your agency.

As a community organizer dependent on grants to fund your programs, you always have to worry about the funding sources drying up. If they do, you have to be exceptionally creative and resourceful to compete with others for that community service dollar.

DEGREE REQUIREMENTS

Not only is the MSW necessary for administrative jobs, but you are also expected to have state licensure with specialization in social work administration.

For the community organizer, it is essential that you have your MSW and broad experience in social work administration and community organization.

OPPORTUNITIES IN THE FIELD

The field, particularly for community organizer social workers, is dependent on the economic climate. When times are tough and service programs are being cut, it is harder to get funds for projects.

Men and women are usually evenly distributed in these jobs. Men naturally gravitate toward the more financially rewarding positions in the field, and some of those positions are seen as an extension of the corporate world. You need assertiveness, shrewd business sense, and initiative—traits that are traditionally ascribed to men.

You also need patience and resourcefulness because things rarely go the way you've planned. An aggressive attitude may appeal to your supervisors who see things getting done, but your subordinates will resent that attitude. You won't accomplish much without their cooperation.

Women do make good administrators, but, as in many professions, men seem to rise faster in the ranks.

OPPORTUNITIES FOR ADVANCEMENT

In these positions the sky is the limit for advancement. You can go from supervising your department to running the whole agency or another company of equal size.

Community organizers can tackle any size job if they put their mind to it, and because they write their own budgets and find their own funding sources, they can write their own salaries. With each project's success you establish your credentials, so that you can tackle bigger projects. In the end, you may effectively write yourself into a job at a regular agency and then rise to administer that program.

Opportunities for advancement are limited only by your energy and drive.

HOW TO BREAK INTO THE JOB

You need to specialize in social work administration and planning or community organization when working on your MSW degree. Some people have stepped into administrative jobs directly after graduation, but that is unusual. Others have created a niche for themselves by working on a special community project within an agency and then moving on to administrative work after developing planning skills.

Read everything you can about communities to gain a thorough knowledge of the good ones and the bad—and why. Take some business courses, courses on your department's research methods, and city and regional planning courses. Learn all you can about grant writing and applying for other funding sources. Even as an administrator, you will be expected to bring money into the agency.

If you cannot find a suitable spot right away, take any related position and develop your community proposals in your spare time. Get on the board of some organization in your community. I became a trustee at the library and was surprised how quickly I made vital contacts in the community.

When you have established your name in the community, you can activate your own network system. If you don't hear about the perfect job, you may just have to create it.

HELPFUL HINTS ON THE JOB

1. Be professional, because you are highly visible in these roles.
2. Remember your friends and contacts. You got where you are through hard work and other people's support.
3. Learn to manage your time efficiently; otherwise there won't be enough hours in the day.
4. Subscribe to all pertinent journals.
5. Hold to your principles; they are your most important assets.

EAP (Employee Assistance Program) Social Worker

Salary range: $30,000 and up, depending on locale and size of agency. An entry-level position would likely be in the mid-twenties.

JOB DESCRIPTION

Employee Assistance Program (EAP) social workers discussed here are the "in-house" social workers who are hired by the organization that they serve and are therefore part of the organization. Other social workers provide EAP services that are external to the companies served; they are discussed in chapter 12.

Employee Assistance Programs evolved out of the early substance-abuse field. Managers needed to find some way to help the employee who was no longer doing an effective job because of chronic tardiness, absenteeism, or a poor attitude. Substance-abuse workers, who were usually recovering alcoholics or addicts, demonstrated to employers that the alcoholic employee could be rehabilitated and put back on the job—at a saving to the company, which was losing money because of sick leave costs and the employee's reduced effectiveness on the job. With management behind the programs, the EAPs steadily gained favor; currently some 70 percent of Fortune 500 companies have EAPs in place. By encouraging the employee to do something constructive about his problem, the companies saved money. If the employee resolved his drinking problem (which was the primary focus in the beginning of EAP work), he returned to his job and presumably became more efficient.

Today, the focus of EAPs has broadened to include any personal problems that are causing the employee trouble on the job: finances, the state of a marriage, a family member's drug problems, or legal difficulties. Some in-house Employee Assistance Programs help resolve work-related stress, or friction between employer and employee. Many companies believe that if they are going to uncover employee problems on the job (and with mandatory drug-testing more problems are being uncovered), they must have a program to help the employee. Hence the increasing reliance on already established EAPs.

One part of the EAP social worker's job is to counsel the people he serves. He does an intake on the person asking for services to decide what type of service is needed. If the EAP social worker cannot provide the service himself—if more in-depth clinical counseling is needed—he or she refers the person to a qualified social worker in the community. Sometimes, however, the EAP social worker continues to provide individual or marital counseling to the employee. Since this service is free to the employee in the work setting, he or she is more apt to take advantage of it.

In addition to counseling, the EAP social worker acts as a consultant to supervisors (or may do so if his job description permits it). In this role he offers advice on work-related difficulties with employees and does problem-solving with the supervisors to resolve crises with the least disruption. One EAP social worker in a university says that supervisors call him asking for suggestions on how to approach an employee on a work-related issue. He recommends addressing the problem behavior—not the character of the employee—and then suggests how that behavior can be improved.

A third aspect of EAP work is training other personnel in better work relations. The social worker does this by preparing and conducting workshops for other in-house staff. (An example might be: How to Manage Difficult People.)

As the EAP social worker becomes recognized in the field, he or she is sought out as a speaker at conferences. Depending on where you are asked to deliver your workshop and how you are compensated for the extra job, you may end up with a paid vacation.

EAP social workers also provide job counseling, career counseling, and referral services—they even help an employee find a good lawyer if that is needed. He or she may be asked to help an employee "fit in better" on the job. Many times a person gets a job without knowing how to conduct himself. He may not know how to dress, how to talk politely to his peers or supervisors, or even how to present himself in public. It is usually assumed that a potential employee knows that stuff. Not knowing it, however, creates stress on the job—for the supervisor, the employee, and all those who work with him. Then it is the social worker's job to help, because the supervisor does not have time.

The work of the EAP social worker is usually of a short-term nature unless he has a private practice and can see employees for ongoing clinical counseling. At the workplace, however, the EAP social worker handles a variety of problems, stepping in to smooth things between supervisor and employee so that work can continue.

The Good Points
One of the good points of this job is the diversity of tasks. My friend Shaun, who works at the University of Southern Maine, told me, "I get to have a lot of fun in

this job. I don't just sit in an office. That's a small part of what I do."

Your day will not be structured. Although you have to respond to supervisors who contact you about a problem, how you respond is up to you.

One of the good things about an in-house setting is that you are observed by everyone in the organization and are therefore more readily accepted than an outsider. If you are good at your job, many people will appreciate what you do—not only for them, but for the agency as well. You can feel good about the changes you make in an individual and realize that you have helped the organization keep a valued employee.

Seeing constructive changes result from your efforts is a real plus; being appreciated for them is an added bonus.

You can experience a high degree of success in this job. In part, that is because you deal with high-functioning people. (Someone who has gotten a job is functioning at a higher level than the severely disturbed person who cannot hold a job.) Likewise, you work with people who are more inspired to do something about their problems. Knowing that he risks losing his job if he does not get help, the employee is more motivated than someone who is inclined to quit when the going gets tough.

Another reason you see more success in this job is that some of your successes will be small ones—for example, linking the employee to another service in the community. Nonetheless, every gain made is a success, and you don't feel so drained at the end of the day when you have done something that others appreciate.

Other good points about this job are the salary, which is good, and the opportunities for growth, which are tremendous.

The Disadvantages

If you are not a high-energy person, this is not the job for you. It is not a job where you can sit in your office all day waiting for people and problems to come to you. You have to keep your files updated with resources in the community. You will have to make yourself visible and get a feel for your organization. People have to know you are there before they will come to you for help.

No supervisor will tell you how to do your job. If you cannot structure your own day, you will not enjoy this job—nor will you be good at it.

Problem-solving can be tiring, especially when you are working with people (supervisors or employees) who see no need to change. You will experience mishaps in this work, as in other clinical fields, and part of handling the job is learning to accept that you cannot help everyone.

Some people worry that office politics will make EAP work unpleasant—that management will not appreciate your efforts if they think you always consider them the problem. According to my friend in this field, politics are rarely as troublesome as social workers fear it will be. Most organizations realize that the EAP worker is performing a needed service that is cost-effective in the long run.

The paperwork and hours may seem burdensome, but there is plenty of paperwork in all social work positions, and the hours are what you make of them. If you spend more than is stipulated in your contract, either you are not working efficiently or there is more work than one person can handle. If you start accommodating a company that wants fifty hours of work for forty hours' pay, you are setting a dangerous precedent.

Degree Requirements

Believe it or not, there are no special educational requirements at this time. That is likely to change before you get out of college, however, because all professional jobs are requiring greater specialization these days.

Because the original EAP workers were substance-abuse counselors who were recovering from their own addiction, they seldom had specialized degrees in counseling. As the program broadens to include tasks outside the realm of drug and alcohol abuse, candidates with experience in clinical counseling are needed. Increasingly, MSWs are filling the void because of their systems approach and greater knowledge of community resources.

The Employee Assistance Professionals Association has its own credentials. It offers licensing as a Certified Employee Assistance Professional by spending a certain number of hours of certified supervision (which means working in apprenticeship with a Certified EAP), and passing a national exam. Common sense suggests that you need clinical experience, and that comes through working in a psychiatric setting, like a hospital or an agency, where you need an MSW. Save yourself time and regrets by getting your Master's degree at the outset.

OPPORTUNITIES IN THE FIELD

In-house EAP jobs are on the rise as companies discover how economical they are. Therefore, the field is not saturated, even though the mental-health agencies and private clinicians may have a hold on the external EAP programs. However, the jobs are not always advertised.

Women dominate in this area only because more women have MSWs. It is likely, however, that men will gravitate to the field when they realize the challenges it offers.

OPPORTUNITIES FOR ADVANCEMENT

Depending on the size of the company or organization, this job offers some potential for advancement. If you are part of a large Human Resources department you can move up the ladder.

Otherwise, the opportunities for advancement in this position are lateral. You can move to another company for more money or prestige, but within the corporation there is no way up unless you move into another line of work.

How to Break into the Job

Most EAP jobs are not listed in the newspapers because companies like to have a candidate in mind before they establish their in-house program. That is where networking is important. If your skills are known and respected in the community, you may be consulted about a job before you know a job is being offered.

Keep in mind, however, this is not an entry-level job in which candidates fresh out of college can be effective. You need to "pay your dues," so to speak, by gaining clinical experience, and one of the best places to do that is in a psychiatric setting. Working in a counseling agency is instructive, but the fastest way to pick up clinical skills is in a psychiatric hospital. Working in an admissions area, assessing the problems that come through, and dealing with the more severe forms of mental illness will strengthen your skills. In hospital work you also learn how to behave professionally. When you have acquired some experience (and that includes diplomatic skills), you can activate your networking leads to discover the right EAP job.

Work in a personnel agency while in school, or in addition to any social work job you may have. In that way you can start out with a knowledge of how organizations work and the Human Resources department in particular.

Even if you have your MSW degree, you might consider an apprenticeship program with a Certified

Employee Assistance Professional. You will end up with your CEAP certificate and many job leads.

Know your material. Read not only about EAPs but also about organizational structure. Take some business courses. Find out why Lee Iacocca turned his organization around, and why Trump fell out of favor.

HELPFUL HINTS ON THE JOB

1. Read all the EAP journals you can get your hands on. Some are expensive, so see if your company will order them for your department. Here are some choices:

   EAP Association Exchange (monthly)
   EAP Association, Inc.
   4601 North Fairfax Drive
   Arlington, VA 22203

   Employee Assistance (monthly)
   225 North New Road
   Waco, Texas 76710

   EAP Digest (bimonthly)
   Performance Resource Press
   2145 Crooks Road
   Troy, MI 48084

2. Get to know the company's supervisors, and don't assume you are there only to address the "little man's" needs. Be careful not to prejudge any situation.
3. Practice professionalism; respect confidentiality.
4. Keep your community resources file active. Maintain your old contacts and consistently make new ones.
5. Enjoy your work; if you don't, what's the point?

10

Family Planning Clinic Social Worker

Salary range: $15,000 to $28,000, depending on the agency's funding sources and your credentials and experience. Private agencies, as a rule, pay more.

JOB DESCRIPTION

The social worker can perform numerous tasks in a family planning clinic. Obviously, a great part of her day is spent providing reproductive information to families and counseling people for whom pregnancy is an undesired or unexpected event.

Entry-level social workers (or students fulfilling their practicums) administer pregnancy tests and provide information about pregnancy and health care should the tests be positive. More experienced social workers with clinical skills provide the follow-up counseling if the pregnancy is not a welcomed event.

Family planning agencies vary in their stance on abortion. In some agencies (especially those with a religious affiliation), the social workers do not consider abortion for clients; if a client seeks that specific information they strongly suggest reconsideration. At other agencies, social workers present all alternatives to pregnancy, leaving the decision to the client.

Dealing with teenage clients in a highly charged emotional situation has to be carefully done. Because many clients are under eighteen, and because some communities object to providing abortion information to anyone, the family planning social worker needs to be sensitive to opinions in the community. You should know your own values first and foremost. The social worker cannot direct people to do things she considers unethical.

The U.S. Supreme Court declared abortion legal in 1973 in the landmark case *Roe v. Wade*. Over the past years, pro-life advocates have lobbied long and hard to get the Court to reverse itself. Legislation during the administrations of both Ronald Reagan and George Bush did succeed in limiting women's rights to abortion. In May 1991, the Court upheld a ruling that clinics receiving Title X government funds cannot provide abortion information or referrals for abortions to pregant women. Every pregnant woman, no matter what her age or circumstance, must be referred for prenatal care. That meant that only women who could afford an abortion at a privately funded clinic retained their right to an abortion. The ruling clearly discriminated against poor women. Not only could these women not get an abortion at the clinics, but they could not even be referred to places that would perform the abortion. Obviously, the ruling presented a dilemma to many social workers who subscribe to the NASW Code of Ethics, which says:

"The social worker should act to ensure that all persons have access to the resources, services, and opportunities which they require."

Social workers were forced to be quite "creative" in order to block abortion. They needed to learn how to deal with such escalating tensions while continuing to provide the same services for all their clients. Some simply resigned from their jobs.

In January 1993 (exactly twenty years after *Roe. v. Wade*), President Bill Clinton took office and lifted the gag order on clinics receiving Title X funds. As of today, federally funded clinics may once again provide abortion information to their clients. A pro-choice President will help ensure that abortion remains a legal option for women. NASW is obviously pro-choice. Its policy statement says: "Women's right to choose is consistent with the principles that form the bedrock of social work: self-determination, empowerment, and dignity." (Bear in mind, of course, that not all social workers belong to NASW or endorse its views. You can be a social worker and have a pro-life stance.)

Good and bad news surrounds the abortion controversy. While fewer restrictions may sound good (especially if you are pro-choice), the battles are only heating up. In March 1993, Dr. David Gunn was shot and killed in Pensacola, Florida, for performing abortions. If you choose to work in a family planning clinic that offers abortion services, be prepared to deal with hecklers who target both those seeking abortion and those providing the service. Even though you are not a doctor performing the actual abortion, the fact that you work in such a clinic makes you vulnerable. As conservatives watch erosion of the gains they have made in recent years, they will undoubtedly intensify their efforts.

Whatever your position, you must believe in what you are doing. Whether you are pro-choice or anti-abortion, you must maintain your compassion for the client who has to make the decision. What impressed me most about my colleague who advised against abortion at her clinic was that she continued to work with those clients who nonetheless went elsewhere for the abortion. She found that no matter how prepared the woman was for ending the pregnancy, she still felt pain over the loss. The pain may not flare up immediately, but years later, when something happens to remind her of the previous loss (perhaps another pregnancy or an anniversary date), she is surprised at the hurt from the original loss. In response to that need, this family planning social worker offers a post-abortion recovery group, which is a twelve-week program that allows the women to get in touch with their loss and make peace with themselves. This support group seeks to heal the women, not blame them.

The family planning social worker, then, counsels all clients and refers some to other parts of the health community if necessary. Sometimes she recommends doctors; sometimes she helps a young girl tell her parents that she is pregnant. If an unwed, young mother-to-be needs shelter or financial help, the social worker assists her in connecting with those resources. If the client wants to give her child up for adoption, the social worker provides ongoing counseling to be sure that the woman is emotionally prepared for that experience. Some agencies offer an adoption support group for women in all stages of the adoption process.

Sometimes this social worker provides longer-term counseling for a client who seems particularly at a loss about how to deal with her pregnancy. Clients exhibiting severe signs of mental disorder are referred to the appropriate mental-health facilities, but the family planning social worker provides ongoing counseling to many clients because her services are usually free.

Apart from counseling, the social worker sometimes instructs her clients about their pregnancy (how to care for themselves, how to care for their newborn baby, how to handle the surprises of labor and delivery) and oversees foster home families who support the agency.

At one agency, the head of the department created and managed an outreach program for rural clients who could not come in for family planning services. She arranged to have a social worker visit these young women, making sure they knew that they could finish their education in an alternative program if not at their regular high school. She referred some to Human Services and provided guidance for others regarding care for the newborn.

Some social workers run homes for unwed mothers and programs to link foster families with either pregnant teenagers or with their babies on a temporary basis. The social worker is responsible for matching the families and monitoring their care.

Some social workers who start out in these clinics eventually create their own programs, funded by the parent agency or through special community grants. One woman set up her own alternative high school program for teenage mothers, staffing it with licensed teachers, school nurses, and day-care providers.

THE GOOD POINTS

This job is never boring either, because people come in all shapes and sizes and with all kinds of problems. You have so many tasks to accomplish at any given time that you should have no opportunity to get bored.

Working closely with families struggling over major decisions can be gratifying when you succeed in helping them. Successes can be small, but nevertheless satisfying. All some people need is information. Some need advice; some need referrals. These services should be easy to supply, and your efforts will be appreciated.

Helping to develop a more responsible person and a more caring parent is gratifying too. If through your efforts a person learns to cope with her predicament, you will feel good about your contribution.

THE DISADVANTAGES

Because you work in stressful situations, this work can be tiring. The small successes make this giving "tolerable," but it is the distress and failures that may shorten your time spent in this kind of work. Being around so much pain can be draining.

Dealing with the political repercussions of some of your informational services (particularly abortion referrals) is also draining. I don't think people who go into this line of work do so with the intent of taking a forceful stand on any one issue, but sometimes that is what happens.

The pay is low, relatively speaking, unless you manage the agency and assume additional roles. If you do not provide direct services, it means overseeing the volunteers or other social workers who do and being ultimately accountable for their actions.

DEGREE REQUIREMENTS

For some of those jobs you can be a volunteer (while working on your MSW or BSW degree), but because of the nature of the work you are well advised to obtain your MSW. Many students opt to spend their practicums on the job, gaining experience by learning how to integrate what they hear in the classroom with what goes on in the real world.

For those in counseling positions (where good clinical skills are needed), the MSW is required. Those with BSWs can run some of the support groups. Some agencies require the MSW and state licensure anyway. Since all social work positions are moving toward specialization, the candidate for family planning social worker would be wise to educate him or herself as much as possible. If one decides to add other aspects of social work (for example, teaching courses in social work and supervising practicum students), one definitely needs the MSW degree and licensure.

OPPORTUNITIES IN THE FIELD

These jobs are often filled by new social workers or volunteers (still in school), so there may be more social workers who can do the work than there are funds or positions.

As you can probably guess, more women fill these roles than men.

Because the pay is relatively low, there is considerable turnover as entry-level social workers gain experience and move on to jobs with more challenge and financial compensation.

OPPORTUNITIES FOR ADVANCEMENT

Since social workers can start in entry-level positions or as volunteers, there is plenty of room to advance. As you gain experience and the necessary credentials, you can move into counseling roles and eventually advance to an administrative position if your agency is of sufficient size.

Some social workers combine other aspects of social work and write grant proposals to fund their own projects. Branching out in this capacity—being a consultant as well as an organizer—can be rewarding both financially and personally.

HOW TO BREAK INTO THE JOB

This job is easier to access than some other social work positions because agencies offer entry-level jobs in this area. You can probably walk into a job right out of college if you have the right credentials and some experience in family planning work.

You can gain the experience by either completing your practicum and placements at these agencies or by volunteering during vacations and school breaks. Some tasks, such as administering pregnancy tests and making referrals to other agencies for services, you can do right from the start.

If you want to spend more time in counseling, brush up on your clinical skills first. Work in close supervision with another MSW, or work at a hospital, honing your clinical and assessment skills.

Keep your network channels open. Sometimes these jobs are filled by word of mouth.

If you cannot find a job to your liking right away, take another satisfactory position, but volunteer at one of these agencies in the meantime. When an opening occurs, the staff may offer it to you because they are familiar with your work.

HELPFUL HINTS ON THE JOB
1. Respect the client's confidentiality at all times.
2. Respect the values of your agency. If you cannot condone some of its practices, it is best not to work there; compromising your values to make a living will eat away at your self-esteem.
3. Read everything in the field. Ask your agency to subscribe to the major journals, or order them yourself.
4. Stay on top of community resources; like information, resources are always changing.

Social Work Instructor

Salary range: $28,000 to $70,000, depending on the college or university and on your experience and credentials.

JOB DESCRIPTION

Since social work is not a subject taught in high school, this chapter addresses college level instructors.

Depending on the size of the college and its social work department, an instructor is responsible for any number of tasks. First and foremost, the instructor has to prepare the course, deliver the lectures or lead discussions, devise a way (usually by test or essay) to assess what the student has learned, and then grade the work. Readying yourself to teach a course in social work is no easy matter. You have to know your subject, and that means immersing yourself in it so that you have more information than what is in the textbooks. Sometimes you may be able to choose the textbooks for the course. But teaching goes beyond knowing the material. It requires the ability to make the subject understandable to others. Thus you need to be an entertainer and a disciplinarian.

To be a good instructor, you must be open to even more learning. You will spend a great deal of time getting to know your students, because the better rapport you have with them, the easier it is to engage them in class. Also, administering tests and grading papers takes a lot of time.

Part of social work instruction is monitoring work practicums, coordinating placements in the community, and getting input from the supervisors under whom the students work. (Not all instructors fill this role, however.) As a field instructor, you continually have to drum up "good" placements; you spend a lot of time checking in with the supervisors and monitoring the student's work. If problems crop up, it is your job to smooth them out. Whether that means taking the student in hand or helping the supervisor get along better with the student, it calls for diplomacy.

Part of an instructor's job is to promote the image of his college or university, and that means committee work, "hobnobbing" with the public to generate community support, and attending university functions.

Many instructors act as counselors, although that is not their designated role. Good teachers always do more than teach; they sometimes sit down with students and help them sort out their troubles so they can get on with their studies. Sometimes instructors refer students to the school's counseling center for advice on many subjects outside their realm. Some college instructors may invite the whole class home for dinner and discussion after class.

Instructors often help a student decide on life goals. It may be easier for the student to talk to a teacher he or she trusts than to a guidance counselor who seems to be a stranger.

When instructors are noted in their field, they may be asked to speak at organizations or to conduct workshops in their field of expertise. You need to perfect your speaking ability because you cannot rely on your authority as a teacher to carry you through these large gatherings. Nowhere is a sense of humor more appreciated. People who attend workshops want to learn something, of course, but they also want to be entertained. A good instructor can do both.

THE GOOD POINTS

Being an instructor offers you independence (although you still have to conform to your school's policies) and challenge. You work with idealistic young students who typically want to "change the world," and their enthusiasm is catching at times.

In this position, you get to share your ideas and have the satisfaction of seeing people take notes on what you say. You are an authority figure, and others will look up to you. You direct the flow of the classroom and create your own evaluation tools. Being appreciated and fondly remembered—what greater pleasure is there?

As a rule, you are well paid as an instructor and have the opportunity to travel when attending workshops. You have ample breaks in your schedule and a lengthy summer vacation. If you are a tenured professor, you have periodic sabbaticals when you can use a whole semester (with pay) to go somewhere else and research your next book—or teach in another university.

Being an instructor has numerous "perks." Your children can attend your college either at a reduced fee or for free. Other colleges may offer reduced fees to your children as a professional courtesy. You have the opportunity to influence the direction of your department and to make a lasting contribution in your field of specialization.

THE DISADVANTAGES

Now the bad stuff. You must be prepared to teach each class, even when you don't feel like preparing a lecture the night before. It takes a lot of time to prepare a lecture and to study enough other material to remain an authority on the subject. Not only that, but you have to devise tests and course assignments and read papers. That takes a substantial amount of time. Fairly assessing someone's work—for example, making relevant notes in the margins—takes time, and the only time you have is after hours, when the students have gone home.

Students will expect you to make the course not only understandable, but also entertaining. They expect you to be knowledgeable, funny, and sometimes as idealistic as they are. Because you are an authority figure, however, they will reject some of what you say.

Your hours extend far beyond the classroom. You may have to explain the systems theory to a student for the umpteenth time because he just hasn't "gotten" it. You might have to calm another student who thinks she's going to flunk your research and methods course. And you have to stand firm when still another student suggests that you gave him a C- on his exam because he is foreign and you are prejudiced.

If the students don't wear you down, the politics of the department just might. Trying to teach a subject while being sensitive to the public image of the college can be tiresome. Some instructors say that committee work is the most boring aspect of their job.

DEGREE REQUIREMENTS
In this profession you need two types of degrees. At the minimum, of course, you need the MSW degree. With that you are eligible to teach in some junior colleges (two-year programs of study) and some of the smaller colleges. In a major university, however, you need both the MSW and the PhD (or DSW). Instructors in the larger universities usually hold a PhD, because teaching requires greater and greater specialization.

OPPORTUNITIES IN THE FIELD
Sources say the need for instructors in social work is great. As usual, more women are visible in the field.

However, as many males as females earn a PhD, so the profession of teaching in the larger universities is probably evenly divided between the sexes.

No matter what people say, men still rise faster within the ranks, perhaps because they do not have the interferences that women may face during the child-bearing years.

In teaching, as long as you have the right credentials you can usually find a job, although you may have to relocate for it. Then, as you demonstrate your capabilities, you can either find a more secure position in another college or be accepted as an assistant professor and then professor in your current school.

OPPORTUNITIES FOR ADVANCEMENT

As long as you are willing to go as far as you can in your education by obtaining your PhD (which means an additional two to three years of schooling beyond your MSW) you have plenty of opportunity for advancement. One starts out as an instructor at a college or university, then rises to assistant professor, full professor, and tenured professor, which means not having to negotiate a contract each year. If you cannot rise any higher at your current university, you can look elsewhere; as long as you are willing to relocate, you have plenty of choices available.

As long as you are an effective teacher, publish something of professional interest every few years, and maintain an untarnished public image, you can stay in the field for as long as you choose, perhaps even heading the department if the chance presents itself.

HOW TO BREAK INTO THE JOB

You can break into this field in one of three ways. First, you can make a name for yourself even while you're in school, working on your Master's degree and teaching courses in the undergraduate program. As you work on your PhD, you can teach master's-level courses so that when you graduate and are ready to start teaching full time the school is familiar with your work and may have an opening for you.

A second way is to take a regular social work job once you have your MSW and learn all you can about a certain position (for example, clinical social work). After a period of time you return to school for an additional degree (the PhD or DSW) to enable you to parlay your practical experience and your degrees into a teaching position. Someone who has actually worked in the "real" world has more to offer than someone with only book knowledge, however grand that might be.

A third way is to get all your education upfront but then go directly into a profession. While you're working as a social worker—no matter what kind—you can sign on to teach "supplemental" courses in social work at night, for example. That may mean teaching introductory-level courses, but as you gradually make a name for yourself and free up more of your time, you can make the transition to full-time teaching if the opening arises.

If your goal is to teach (and believe me, most people choose to go into this profession; they don't end up teaching because they couldn't do anything else), you should take as many educational courses as you can fit into your schedule. Take a Dale Carnegie course to improve your speaking ability and assertiveness. You have to be able to sell yourself to get the job in the first place and to keep classroom attention.

Volunteer to teach a Sunday or Hebrew school class while you're a student; you'll get a feel for holding kids' attention and some sense of how to plan lessons—even those you don't have to grade.

Talk to your college instructors; they can give you

valuable ideas on how to pursue your goals and act as references later.

Having taught classes in Sociology (a related field) and been a clinical social worker, I think you have far more to offer the student if you have been out in the real world, seeing how the social worker lives and works, before you attempt to teach others what it's like.

Applying for a position, putting yourself (your credentials and experience) in a positive light, and calling in those references will eventually land you a good job.

HELPFUL HINTS ON THE JOB

1. Never allow yourself to grow stale while teaching; always keep learning yourself.
2. Make yourself available to the students; that's what you're there for.
3. Realize the limits of your job; you don't have to be a counselor if you don't have the skills.
4. Stay in touch with the fields you teach; nothing is worse than presenting yourself as an authority if you aren't one.
5. Support your college and your colleagues by attending school functions. And enjoy yourself; if you don't (as I've said before), what's the point?

Human Services Department Social Worker

Salary range: $15,000 to $28,000. The higher figure represents salaries for administrators or department heads.

JOB DESCRIPTION

I could devote a whole book to this aspect of social work alone, so broad and varied are the jobs in the Human Services Department. Years ago, the traditional social worker in this department did all the jobs in his designated locale. When I worked as an intern for the Department of Health and Welfare, I handled clients who were awaiting their monthly AFDC (Aid to Families with Dependent Children) checks; I assisted other social workers in removing children from homes considered temporarily unfit; I sat in on court sessions where a child's custody was being disputed; and I reviewed families who were applying to be foster parents. Any welfare business that occurred in the area fell into my domain. I was the trusty welfare social worker who trekked around meeting my people in their homes.

That has mostly changed. Even as I was returning to school after my internship, the rules were changing. Now social workers specialize in certain tasks, which means that some people handle adoption procedures, some handle foster families, and some handle juvenile services. In almost all agencies (with the possible exception of small rural agencies that have retained the traditional social worker's tasks), you have a specific job to perform in the Human Services Department. Human Services is the largest social service agency in each state, and the social workers there are responsible for coordinating all state family services and the lives of thousands of welfare recipients.

If you work in adoption services, you are responsible for coordinating the paperwork that goes along with giving a child up for adoption as well as offering short-term counseling to the mother who is relinquishing her parental rights. It means overseeing the adoption court procedures, assessing the emotional and physical health of the prospective parents (as well as their resources), and following up on both families once everything has been signed and agreed upon.

In this agency, you do not handle one case at a time; the Department of Human Services is always swamped with families needing services. You handle scores of cases, all in various stages of development.

The same thing is true if you work in foster care placement. You typically have an unwieldy caseload. You will have the unpleasant task of separating families, even those who can't stand to be around each other. For most kids, even the worst parents are better than strangers. Most children resist being taken (even temporarily) from their home and placed in foster care. I remember helping another social worker who had to transport three children under the age of twelve to a foster home while their mother was hospitalized for surgery. Since the new home would be calmer and had loving parents, I wasn't prepared for the protests that filled the back seat of our car. The kids didn't care that they'd be getting their own rooms and a pile of toys. All they knew was that they were being taken from their home—even though their mother was not necessarily considerate or loving.

In foster care work you also have to follow up on your support families—those people who agree to take in foster kids. It is your responsibility to be sure they are adequate substitute parents themselves and that they are using the state's money to support the foster children, not themselves. You'll spend time assessing families, matching needy children with potential parents, and attempting to keep the paperwork pileup to a minimum. You may get to do some individual counseling with foster children, but you should not consider yourself a clinical social worker. You may be expected to refer a person to a mental-health center for counseling—and then provide transportation to appointments.

Some social workers specialize in court-related community services, acting as probation and parole counselors with juveniles. In this job the social worker (or caseworker, as he or she is sometimes called) offers in-home counseling to the adolescent and his family, accompanies the offender to court, presents reports to the judge, and helps to place some adolescents in private or state facilities as needed.

Some social workers focus on helping recipients of welfare assistance to develop job skills and eventually become employable. Although social workers do not make the routine "home visits" they formerly made, they still make periodic visits to the clients' homes to make sure they are "playing by the rules."

Some social workers have the difficult job of investigating child abuse—verifying that abuse has occurred (which means following up on all reports of abuse), rescuing the child from the home, and then representing the child's interests in court.

In all these jobs you develop your assessment and referral skills. You do not do in-depth clinical counseling, however; that job is better reserved for the clinical social worker, who is discussed in chapter 14.

THE GOOD POINTS

These jobs are offered to the entry-level social worker, so while you are not necessarily paid a large salary, you will have a job. Another plus: These jobs are relatively easy to transfer into if you move to another state.

Many of the jobs are gratifying. Not only are you doing work that is needed in the community, but many people are actually appreciative of your efforts. You have the opportunity to make a difference in people's lives; sometimes you'll have to intervene in life-threatening situations. The successes justify the headaches.

You'll have a chance to perfect your assessment skills, because you are expected to perform a variety of tasks in addition to the referrals you make. The knowledge acquired from this job will help you in all other social work positions if you choose to move into another area.

THE DISADVANTAGES

Many of these jobs offer some degree of danger. People do not always appreciate your services, particularly when you intervene in their lives, telling them what they can and cannot do. Of course, the law is on your side, but some people still won't care. In some areas you will be considered harsh for sticking your nose into private affairs. There are still people who believe that whatever they do in their own family (including the abuse of their kids) is none of your business. When you work with criminals and abusive personalities, you run the risk of being hurt yourself.

Except for administrative positions, these jobs are low-paying, and the only "perks" are travel expenses.

Then, too, you will have more people seemingly "against" you than "for" you. Your supervisors may be on your back to hand in your paperwork and document your transactions. At the same time, the public tends to blame Human Services for whatever goes wrong in the handling of clients.

And, as always, the hours can be long, and the paperwork mountainous.

DEGREE REQUIREMENTS

Because many of these jobs are entry level, you can probably start out with only a BSW or a BA (or MA) in a related field. (A related field means any of the social sciences or people-oriented professions.)

The middle-level jobs and, of course, administrative positions require greater specialization, which means an MSW. My sources tell me that to do an official home study in the Human Services department, you have to have your MSW degree.

Although not all of these jobs currently require the advanced degree, it is worth pursuing anyway. You might take an entry-level job and then arrange for the department to send you back to school for the MSW. Human Services, in particular, spends a great deal of money sending its people for advanced training. You don't have to repay the money spent on your education; you merely have to put in two more years of service—for which you'll be paid, of course.

OPPORTUNITIES IN THE FIELD

Turnover is high in these positions, which are often used as springboards for other jobs. There may be a good number of caseworkers for every job, but the chance of being hired is good if you are persistent and patient.

Again, the field is saturated with women because they make up the bulk of those with the MSW degree. Women have traditionally been the "social workers," or helpers, so it is not surprising to find so many still performing that function. Men, however, are a welcome addition to the force.

OPPORTUNITIES FOR ADVANCEMENT

Opportunities for advancement are plentiful, usually because you are starting at the entry level. Also there is an enormous range of jobs in the department. If you rise to head any department, you then have the opportunity to branch out into administrative work in other agencies and organizations.

HOW TO BREAK INTO THE JOB

For all state jobs you have to pass a state merit exam in addition to meeting the degree requirements. When you have your educational experience, you sign up for a variety of social worker I or II positions (whatever level you qualify for) at the state employment (or personnel) office and then take the scheduled exam.

At the state personnel office you'll find a huge book detailing all the state positions and the degree requirements for each. All you have to do is pick out the job that interests you. When you have passed the exam, your name goes onto a register in order of grade. When you're high enough on the list, your name is offered to various supervisors to interview for an opening. You can increase your chances for an interview by getting in touch with various employers yourself, but don't make a nuisance of yourself in this respect.

It helps to do your practicum here, or to work during the summers even in a clerical capacity. The idea is to make yourself known—and indispensable—to the agency so that you will be considered for any appropriate job opening.

HELPFUL HINTS ON THE JOB

1. Respect your clients' dignity. Being needy and desperate makes us all behave badly at times.

2. Keep checking on the state jobs available. Openings come up frequently, and sometimes the person who gets to the supervisor first gets the job.
3. Be sensitive to the politics in your department, and keep documentation of cases current and accurate.
4. Stay on top of your paperwork right from the start.
5. Do your best no matter what your job is. No one will be interested in hiring you for a "better" position if you have not demonstrated that you can handle this one.
6. Remember that you are performing a vital service, even if it does not seem to be appreciated. You are needed, and you should be proud of your contributions.

Department of Corrections Social Worker

Salary range: $25,000-$38,000, varying from state to state.

JOB DESCRIPTION:

There is a difference between the "counselor" with the Department of Corrections and the "mental-health professional." The counselor provides services similar to those of the therapist (discussed in the next chapter), while the mental-health professional handles inmates' problems with the administration and so on.

The clinical social worker for the Department of Corrections works, not surprisingly, in the prison setting. His or her job is to provide regular mental status monitoring (assessing an inmate's mental status—whether he might be having neurological or psychological problems) of all inmates, sitting in on inmate review panels, providing crisis intervention to the inmates, and regular one-on-one therapy or group counseling as needed.

The "counselor" has much more power than a regular clinical social worker in a hospital setting. He can recommend various safety measures (i.e., suicide precautions); only a doctor is needed to request that an inmate be placed in 4-point restraints (all four limbs restrained).

The counselor routinely sees all inmates to do a mental status exam, which is a series of questions to determine clients' memory capacity, attention, and whether or not he is out of touch with reality. Either an inmate can request additional counseling time, or the counselor may recommend that a particular inmate be evaluated further for psychiatric problems. (A staff psychiatrist would prescribe medication.)

The counselor is automatically given ten sessions with an inmate if he requests it. All counseling is topic-specific and time-limited. If the inmate needs further sessions, the counselor recommends such and is usually granted them.

The caseworker makes pardon and parole appearances, acts as disciplinarian when a major rule violation occurs, and makes sure documentation is current and accurate. One caseworker who has held this position says, "The inmates have a level system, and they know exactly what is expected of them, but one of the reasons people come to prison is that they break society's rules. Most of the individual counseling is spent confronting the behaviors that brought them to prison or confronting the behaviors that have prevented them from moving up a level or resulted in their getting dropped a level. Group therapy focuses on value clarification and positive reinforcement; family therapy focuses on establishing a support system for the inmate and setting goals for release. If the family refuses to be involved, or they are unable to be involved because of distance, the inmate is linked up with community resources for additional support."

The correctional counselor works within the prison walls. He has his own office, and inmates may be brought to his office for therapy sessions. In a maximum security prison, the inmate is brought, shackled, to the appointment. If the counselor is comfortable with the idea, the escort (guard) removes the shackles for the duration of the appointment and waits directly outside the office.

Other inmates have to be seen on their units in a private office. Still others, far more dangerous and unreliable, remain in their cells, and the counselor talks to them through an opening in the door (through which they get their meals).

My sources tell me that counselors have plenty of inmates wanting to see them. Prison life is depressing, and inmates often worry about what is happening to their families outside prison. Some inmates additionally have psychiatric problems, and the counselor must assess whether they need medication.

THE GOOD POINTS

As a correctional counselor you have the opportunity to help a variety of men and women cope with one of the most stressful situations imaginable: incarceration.

If you are expected to be on-call on weekends, you rarely need to go out to the prison. You can handle the crises over the phone, so on-call duties are rarely that demanding.

Benefits are good—insurance coverage and vacation and sick leave. Depending on the state, you are well-paid compared to many social work jobs.

Being in a prison setting, you have a captive audience (pun intended). You need not worry whether the inmate will keep his or her appointment unless the guards can't bring him.

A correctional counselor has an important role in helping the inmate cope and has more authority to affect the inmate's life than the average clinical social worker.

Finally, my sources tell me the demand for these social workers will only increase as the number of criminals being incarcerated grows.

THE DISADVANTAGES

This job is often carried out in a tense, hostile atmosphere where incidents of overt violence (not necessarily against you) are commonplace. In other words, it is not a job for the faint of heart. A prison's reason for being is control and security; mental-health concerns are not a high priority and often are seen as a negative by security personnel. Therefore the correctional counselor, who is "low man on the totem pole," so to speak, has to rely on the officers' schedules to escort clients to the office.

Finally, when there is trouble on the ward, everything shuts down and inmates are placed in their cells. The security personnel do not care that an inmate might have an appointment with you. Your schedule is secondary to theirs.

Inmates may threaten to hurt you or your family, even though they are really not in a position to carry out their threats. For that reason, you should not discuss personal things about yourself with inmates, and you should not keep family pictures around your office. Inmates can get away with using foul language in front of counselors, because, after all, what more can officers do to them? Counselors need to be unflappable and yet firm, confident, and thick-skinned.

DEGREE REQUIREMENTS

To be a corrections counselor, you need to be licensed. In order to be licensed, you must have your MSW degree. It is also important to have prior experience in correctional work, whether as a tech or a probation and parole officer.

OPPORTUNITIES IN THE FIELD

There will always be a need for counselors in correctional institutions because the number of criminals being incarcerated is increasing.

More men may be represented in these jobs, mainly because there are more male inmates than female inmates. However, there are no rules stipulating that only men can work in male prisons and only females can work in female prisons. Because of the need to be firm and thick-skinned (traditional attributes ascribed to men), men seem to predominate here.

OPPORTUNITIES FOR ADVANCEMENT

As for advancing in the field, there are not many places to go if you plan to stay in corrections. Some counselors eventually go into private practice, working as therapists. Some contract with the Department of Corrections to provide outpatient services to former inmates, especially those requiring sex-offender treatment. Of course, one can also go into teaching or an administrative position.

HOW TO BREAK INTO THE JOB

My sources tell me it is best to get some experience first in corrections work and in mental-health settings before trying to be a corrections counselor. Starting out as a probation and parole officer or a mental-health professional gives you more insight into the prison population and procedures. You don't need a Master's degree for this kind of work.

Working at a mental-health facility gives you the opportunity to learn about psychiatric disorders as well as the practice of counseling.

Taking parttime jobs or doing social work practicums at these agencies will be helpful in giving you an "in" and exposing you to the type of work you will be doing. Good material to put on your résumé.

Of course, state jobs require you to take the appropriate state tests. Check out the available jobs at the state department and sign up to take the required tests.

HELPFUL HINTS ON THE JOB

1. Develop a thick skin. Many inmates will want to test your mettle by threatening you or cussing in front of you.
2. Make yourself helpful to the staff (the officers). You'll need their cooperation, and one way to secure it is to be helpful first.
3. Keep abreast of therapy practices. Read journals not only to gain knowledge about therapeutic techniques but also about crime and punishment.
4. Your job is not to judge but to serve the clients, in this case, the inmates. Be sure you can put aside your personal values about any crimes they may have committed, and focus on helping them adjust to their situation.
5. Know when to share an inmate's confidences (when self or others may be hurt), and when to keep their secrets.
6. Above all, behave responsibly and professionally. Keep alert at all times, and look for the good in your clients.

Clinical Social Worker/ The Therapist

Salary range: $18,000 to $45,000 (depending on whether your agency is privately funded). Social workers in private practice charge $75 an hour for individual counseling in many areas.

JOB DESCRIPTION
There are innumerable components of clinical social work. Nonetheless, let us take a quick look at some of the tasks and responsibilities of the inpatient social worker (who works in a psychiatric hospital), the outpatient social worker (who works in a mental-health center or private clinic), and the social worker in private practice.

The inpatient social worker in a psychiatric hospital has responsibility for coordinating most aspects of patient care. He or she provides the individual counseling to patients, group therapy to all patients on the ward, family therapy or marital therapy to patients' support systems, and eventual referral to outside agencies for follow-up when patients are released from the hospital.

When I worked at a private psychiatric hospital in Maine, I worked with only five patients at any given time. Perhaps you think that does not sound like much work, but responsibility for those patients meant attending daily doctor rounds and weekly treatment plan meetings (where the staff gets together to put on paper how to treat a case); filling out reports; monitoring the medicine regimens of the patients (and noting whether and how symptoms were subsiding); contacting family members, and either talking to outpatient therapists who had worked with my patients or finding another therapist who would work with them upon discharge. I spent forty to forty-five hours a week doing my job, between the direct service to the patients and the paperwork.

Speaking of paperwork, you have to write initial evaluations and a treatment plan detailing the specific condition you are treating, how you are going to treat it, and how long it should take. Along with these reports, you have to compile an individual and family history. When the patient stays beyond ten days, you have to write another treatment plan indicating why the patient still needs to be hospitalized and offering another discharge date. When the patient is released, you have to write a discharge summary of what transpired in the hospital and where the patient is being referred for outpatient care.

Although the nursing staff takes care of the patient's day-to-day medical needs, as the clinical social worker you are primarily responsible for overseeing his care. Granted, the doctor is ultimately responsible, but he or she delegates this supervision to you, the clinician. The doctor relies on you to report any crisis in the making.

The outpatient social worker has similar responsibilities in that he or she has to fill out the same forms: initial evaluations, treatment plans, and discharge summaries. However, you do not work with the most severely disturbed patients unless it is to refer them to a psychiatric hospital. If you are employed as a case manager, you probably do a lot of work in the community itself, checking up on chronically ill mental patients who are no longer in the hospital. You actually "manage" these clients, because they do not necessarily know how to take care of themselves. That means you have to make sure they are taking their medicine, keeping their other appointments, eating well, and receiving their social security disability checks. If they live in a boarding-house, you need to check with the operator to make sure he or she is taking proper care of your clients or to hear complaints, if any. As a case manager, your job is to help keep the former patient in the community, and to do that you have to monitor all aspects of his or her life and beef up any support systems that may exist. The more supports that are in place for the client, the less direct services you have to perform.

Apart from these tasks, outpatient social workers act much like the social worker in private practice. Your job is to see clients in fifty-minute sessions, providing individual, marital, or family therapy. Counseling is not simply "giving advice." It means listening to the client and helping him or her sort through emotions to find a solution to problems or to find "peace of mind." It does not always happen quickly. People may come to you so depressed that they want to commit suicide. People may come to you because they have just lost their job, their spouse, or their boyfriend or girlfriend. They come because they cannot sleep (or sleep too much); they get stuck thinking the same old thought day after day and can't get anything done; or they come despite being terrified to step outside their door. (These are only a few of the reasons people seek therapy, but you get the idea.) Sometimes you will need to refer your client to a psychiatrist because you suspect that he or she needs medication. Only a psychiatrist can order medication for a client, but that does not mean you have nothing to offer. Medication addresses the biological component of the illness; therapy is still needed because of the months or years of stress built up around the problems.

Some social workers offer psychological treatment for sex offenders who are court-ordered into treatment. Treatment may consist of educational groups, followed by psychotherapy, or just psychotherapy alone. Clinical social workers are usually under contract with the corrections department to offer this service. Because the clients are ordered into treatment and reports of their participation are issued to their probation and parole officers, social workers have more leverage over "reluctant" clients. However, the focus of treatment is not to examine the roots of the sex offender's psychopathology, but rather to educate and prevent the offender from committing another crime.

In a hospital or an agency setting you may be able to offer counseling to another organization as part of an EAP service. You are actually doing the "same old stuff"—but with people from a specific agency or organization.

In private practice in particular, you see some fairly high-functioning clients (as compared to the chronically disturbed former mental patients that one would case-manage in the community, such as schizophrenics and some extreme manic-depressives). Sometimes you have to remind yourself that you are seeing these high-functioning clients to help them, not make tennis dates with them. You cannot blur your boundaries when you are a social worker; friends do not counsel friends. As a professional you must remain objective, and to do that you have to isolate your relationship. (For more information on the therapist's role in treating emotionally disturbed people, read *Coping with Emotional Disorders*. In it we discuss what goes on in therapy from the client's perspective.)

Additionally, the private practitioner has to bill clients, help them fill out insurance forms, write letters on their behalf substantiating a need for treatment, and keep treatment plans and notes accurate and up-to-date.

The clinical social worker or therapist not only supervises other unlicensed—or new—personnel; he or she also receives consultation on his or her cases.

THE GOOD POINTS

Although often very exhausting, therapy is also exhilarating. You can get energized from helping a person sort out his difficulties, and you are rewarded when someone "connects" in a meaningful way with what you are saying. The progress may be miniscule at times, but the successes are still there—and they feel just as good.

Private practice is viewed by those in the field as a lucrative, rewarding way to make a living. You work with higher-functioning people, and you are paid $75 an hour. You sharpen both your clinical skills (you have to be good to survive in this field) and your business sense (since you manage your own practice). Private practice is the "cream of the crop" of clinical jobs.

When you have paid your dues in a psychiatric hospital—particularly if you are good at what you do—your skills are transferable to most of the other jobs. Inpatient work is demanding, varied, and important; if you can be effective in that kind of high-pressure environment you are valuable to a variety of professions. As dim a picture as I may have painted of this social work position, it is very gratifying work. You meet all kinds of people and have the opportunity to make a difference in their lives.

This work is never boring because the human mind is so interesting. I am always fascinated with the resiliency of the human psyche. I learn about myself by helping people sort through the pain in their lives.

In most agencies you receive a stipend (a certain amount of money per year) to spend on work-related conferences or workshops. Depending on the workshop you select, you have the opportunity to create an additional paid vacation, as well as learn with some talented clinicians.

THE DISADVANTAGES

As much as I love this work, it has some serious disadvantages. The work—on very few occasions—is dangerous. People who are hearing voices do not behave predictably. They may believe that you are one of the "bad guys." Sometimes, especially when you must hospitalize a person against his will, you arouse his or her anger. It is not uncommon to get on the wrong side of a divorced spouse, especially when you are working with the other spouse. If you anticipate a potentially dangerous confrontation, make sure you have other people near you or alert the police.

In inpatient work the hours are usually long, the paperwork is excessive, and the pace is frantic. If you can stand up under pressure (and some people actually perform better in those circumstances), you may not find this a liability. Organized people can handle many demands on their time.

Case management is the least desirable position to many clinical social workers, who aspire to be the next "world's greatest therapist." Pay your dues; you will eventually get your chance to branch out on your own, and those former mental patients need you just as much right now.

The salary for case-management positions is low, and the demands on your time are disproportionately greater.

Private practice, as potentially lucrative as it can be, is also unsteady work. There are days when five out of eight clients cancel their appointments or just don't show up. That is a loss of $75 times five, or $375. When you are counting on that money, it's scary when it is not forthcoming. Then there is the unpleasant task of collecting payment from clients who do not intend or cannot afford to pay you.

Clinical social workers who practice in the private sector (and even those working in hospitals and clinics) increasingly have to contend with "third parties." Third parties are usually insurance companies. If you want to get paid for your services (and your clients are not self-paying), you have to submit a claim to their insurance company. Sometimes, EAPs are the third parties. If you want to be reimbursed for seeing their employee, you have to file a claim with them. Third parties affect social workers in two ways. In managed-care situations, third parties seem to dictate the terms of treatment. They decide how long a person should be treated (or at least how long they will pay for treatment). Second, they need to know what's going on with the client to determine how much treatment to authorize. They also expect a diagnosis. Providing a diagnosis to insurance companies is nothing new, but sharing details of treatment with a third party is.

The insurance companies' involvement complicates the client/therapist relationship. After all, to whom does the social worker show his loyalty: the EAP worker who referred the client (and is paying for his treatment), or the client, who is expecting confidentiality? Obviously, it's not clearly defined, but as we see more managed care in the future, we will no doubt see a lessening of the social worker's autonomy and more exceptions to guarantees of confidentiality. If you look on the bright side, however, social workers will end up being accomplished businesspeople as well as therapists. And besides, they are not the only ones dealing with "third parties": doctors and psychologists are in the same boat.

Lastly, holding someone's life in your hands (or feeling as if you do) is exhausting. Sometimes a suicidal patient ends up taking his or her life. Losing a client is wrenching. The little failures—the clients who are having trouble with change—are one thing, but someone's death can feel like the ultimate rejection of your help. It is hard to accept, and it hurts.

DEGREE REQUIREMENTS

To be a case manager (sometimes called a social worker I or Associate) in a state facility, you may need only a BSW and the passing of a state merit exam. In the regular clinical social work positions, however, you need a MSW and state licensure with specialization in clinical practice. Insurance companies do not have to pay health benefits for the services of either unlicensed personnel or those without the MSW. Naturally, no private clinic wants to hire someone for whose services they cannot be reimbursed.

In a hospital setting you can supposedly practice without the MSW as long as you have a master's degree. Even when I was working in such a capacity, the rules were changing. More and more, hospitals prefer to hire MSWs who can be licensed as clinical social workers. You are well advised to get your MSW in the first place.

OPPORTUNITIES IN THE FIELD

Because the more advanced degrees are now being sought, persons with only the BSW or a degree in a related field are being pushed out of these jobs, thereby creating a need for social workers with good clinical skills and the MSW. If you are willing to start in an inpatient setting, you can eventually get a job. There is always a need for dedicated clinical social workers, and the turnover in hospitals is fairly reliable.

As usual, more women are counselors because more women have the MSW. Men in this field often move into administrative roles or private practice. My co-author is one of two male social workers among nine women at a private psychiatric clinic. When I worked in a hospital, there were six clinicians and one male department head. Three of us were women. Since then, one of the men has gone into private practice, one branched out into EAP work at the state university, and the third moved into an administrative position. I left the field, but the two other women remain as clinicians.

OPPORTUNITIES FOR ADVANCEMENT
In this job you have plenty of chances to make more money if you have the right credentials and gain your experience first.

Clinical social workers possess the type of skills needed for a variety of other jobs, including EAP work and organizational service. Improving your skills in the lower-paying jobs enables you to transfer those skills into better-paying positions. You can move laterally into other clinical positions at agencies that pay better (perhaps because of private funding sources), or you can move upward into supervisory positions.

Managing your own private practice or acting as a consultant to organizations are other ways to increase your earnings and satisfy your longing for independence. As long as you have the advanced degree (the MSW or DSW), you can move into various other social work jobs—teaching included.

HOW TO BREAK INTO THE JOB
When you have gone as far in your education as you can afford, you can take one of the appropriate state merit exams to work in a state-run facility (either a mental-health center or a hospital) as a clinical social worker—probably called a Social Worker I, II, III, or higher. As in any other state job, you are placed on a register for that position, and when your name rises

high enough on the list you are sent to a supervisor for an interview. You can increase your chances of getting the job or speed up the process by applying at various agencies. You may start your search with the state employment (or personnel) office where the tests are given, but you should keep checking with specific employers.

During your schooling, spend a field placement in a mental-health agency. Some people have walked into jobs right after college because of their practicums and the contacts they made at those agencies.

You can work as a psychiatric aide at a hospital or mental-health center while you are still in school or after you get out. The pay is minimum wage, but you can't ask for better experience, and the references you can get will help immeasurably in your career pursuits.

Attend NASW meetings; stay in touch with your social work friends from graduate school. When an opening crops up in your field, you want "those in the know" to think of you. Keep your eyes and ears open.

HELPFUL HINTS ON THE JOB

1. Respect the patient's and client's confidentiality. That means not chuckling about someone in the lobby where others might think you're talking about them.
2. Read the current literature in social work and mental health. Research is always presenting new discoveries.
3. Read the journals in your field, even if it means spending an hour or so a week in the library.
4. Behave professionally at all times.
5. Don't be smug. You won't be the world's greatest therapist. Once a client told me that I was the most wonderful therapist in the whole world (which I believed) and that she would

forever be in my debt (which I appreciated). The very next client to walk through my door told me that if I didn't get my act together and give her some real help she wasn't going to come back. That brought me back to earth.

6. Spend more time with your ears open.

7. See the good in your clients, because they probably have no concept of it. Your positive regard for them may be all they are aware of in the beginning. Help them find their strengths.

15

The Case Manager

Salary range: $16,000–$24,000.

JOB DESCRIPTION
In the preceding chapter, you learned that the clinical social worker helps the client to explore and solve his problems. As a therapist, he does not give specific advice or take an overly active role in the client's life.

A case manager is slightly different. While he still serves the client's needs and wants the client to determine those needs, he is more active in helping the client meet those needs. As the title implies, a case manager "manages the client's case."

People with case-management needs are usually lower functioning than therapy candidates. A case manager, for example, will help provide transportation so that his clients can keep all appointments; he may help him file for disability benefits and food stamps because the client is too confused to accomplish this on his own. Case managers, who usually operate out of community mental-health centers, foster care agencies, and hospitals provide more basic services to the client, once it is determined by both the case manager and the consumer (most places prefer to use the term "consumer" than "client") what the consumer wants or needs.

Case managers go through a period of training and supervision in order to be certified for the job. Services performed by certified case managers are reimbursed by the Department of Mental Health and Medicaid, so it's important to obtain the proper training (given on the job).

Sometimes people need both case-management services (help locating housing funds and furnishings) and therapy. The therapist's role precludes going into the community and providing for the client. But it is expected that the bulk of the case manager's work will take place in the community.

An important quality for a case manager is resourcefulness, since your job will often require you to find financial resources for the consumer and to find ways to beef up his support system. Neither case managers nor therapists want to be the consumer's sole support. It is far better for the consumer to find someone or some group in the community to lean on. Social workers find other jobs, move up the ladder into administrative roles, or move away.

THE GOOD POINTS

If you like diversity, you'll like this job because you'll have no set routine. With your caseload, you might be required to make home visits, transport consumers to doctor's appointments, or advocate for them with the Department of Human Services or with their landlords. Your days will be unstructured and varied.

When you accomplish certain specific tasks for your consumer, the results are more obvious. It is rewarding to be able to have such a positive, direct impact on another person's life.

Finally, because of the high turnover in this field, jobs are plentiful.

THE DISADVANTAGES

Having an unstructured day may be a drawback for you, especially if you prefer to sit in your office and let your clients come to you. If you have little initiative, you won't do well here. Case management is meant to take place in the community.

The pay is not good, relative to all your hard work, but it's often an easy place to start out.

In many settings, administrators may set a quota of billable time you should be spending with consumers. Unfortunately, you cannot bill insurance companies or Medicaid simply for transporting a consumer to a necessary appointment. Billable services include times when you are actually advocating for that consumer or linking him/her to some community service. Because so much of what you do cannot be counted as billable service, the administration may feel you're not being productive enough. Just providing supportive counseling is not always considered case management. Having a heavy caseload and trying to keep your time billable can be quite frustrating.

DEGREE REQUIREMENTS
A person needs a bachelor's degree in the mental-health field, with preference given to someone with a BSW. To be certified, one must also get on-the-job training in case management and complete supervision. Each year the certified case manager has to send proof that he has attended "so many hours" of educational workshops to remain certified.

OPPORTUNITIES IN THE FIELD
There are plenty of opportunities here because this is an entry-level position, and there is a great deal of turnover (most likely due to the low pay).

OPPORTUNITIES FOR ADVANCEMENT
There are also plenty of opportunities for advancement, provided the social worker is willing to get more education and training.

Case managers always need supervisors. The higher up you go, the less direct contact with consumers and the more pay.

Many MSW students choose to be case managers while they're working toward their graduate degree. Once they have their MSW, it's easier to move into a therapist position because of their experience.

How To Break into This Job

Once you have your bachelor's degree, peruse the newspapers to see where the openings are—usually with the mental-health centers, hospitals, or foster care agencies. Because the turnover is great, you shouldn't have too much trouble finding an opening.

Use your school practicums to work as an intern at any of these agencies. If you do good work, you'll probably have first rights to the next available job. If you can't do your practicum there, see if you can use the agency as a reference for a term paper (purposely pick a related subject) and spend time getting to know the staff.

If all else fails, volunteer your services (to work in the library, to make appointments, to give clients rides to the agency and back). What you want to do is make a favorable impression on the agency where you'd like to work, so that when there's a job opening, they'll think of you.

Helpful Hints on the Job

1. Be professional and dress the part. Just because you'll be out in the community, don't use that as an excuse to wear play clothes.
2. Keep your appointments as best you can. Crises do come up, but consumers are expecting you to show up at their house when you say you will. If something comes up that is going to make you late for your next appointment, call to notify them.

3. Don't tell the consumer what has to be done; work out a plan together (capitalizing on his or her strengths), and respect the input of the consumer. Try to see things through her eyes.
4. Stay on top of your paperwork, and if you're documenting billable services, make sure your notes reflect actual billable services.
5. Cultivate resources everywhere. The more contacts you have, the more resources you have to work with.

Other Social Work Opportunities

This chapter discusses a variety of other social work positions. Some are quite unusual, and the salary ranges are varied.

One of my friends had been a medical social worker for thirteen years. Saying she felt "unchallenged," she quit her job one spring and joined the Peace Corps as a social worker. She was assigned to a small village in West Africa when her three months of training were over. Georgia Ann had to learn a new language and adjust to a culture quite unlike anything she had ever experienced. In her letter, she wrote: "The sights, sounds, and smells in combination with each other are beyond my imagination."

What did she do in her community site? "My village asked for a village developer to assist in the mobilization of human resources to build a clinic, latrines, wells, chicken coops, and to estimate for other appropriate industries."

As a social worker in the Peace Corps, Georgia Ann earned only a monthly living allotment that wouldn't set her apart from the villagers, and then received a lump sum at the end of service. Her house had no electricity or running water, but she learned firsthand about a different culture and had the opportunity to make a lasting impression on the people. Social workers are, as a rule, good organizers and as such are effective workers for the

Peace Corps. You organize people to build, come together, and improve their basic conditions. The work is both gratifying and backbreaking. It takes incredible courage, patience, and self-sufficiency to take on these jobs. You are away from home for at least two years, with few comforts in your new surroundings.

If you are interested in this kind of work, you do not need an MSW, nor do you need to be a social worker. All you need do is contact the Peace Corps branch in your community and request information. Or you can call 1-800-424-8580, or write to The Peace Corps, 1990 K Street NW, Washington, DC 20526.

It might be useful to get your degree first, however; then you'll have it to fall back on when you have finished your Peace Corps stint. The minimum age is twenty-one years old; there is no maximum age limit. Of those in my friend's training class, some were women in their seventies.

Other similar jobs can be found with the government or military. Your need not join the military to work for them. You can retain your civilian status, but you'll still have to go through strict government procedures and will probably be required to stay for two years' service.

One of the things you should know about these jobs is that you will, undoubtedly, be overworked, because you will be providing counseling services to military personnel. Depending on where you're willing to go, you'll probably find that your services are in high demand. Even if you are not trained in clinical work, you may end up providing therapy because that may be your base's primary need. In some locations, you may find yourself without much support from other social workers, so you need to be independent and self-reliant to do this kind of work. One of our friends who works for the military chose the job because she loves to travel and wanted more contact with a foreign culture. Unfortunately, she doesn't have the time to travel around her beautiful host country, and the only people she sees are American military personnel. Her chief task is providing marital counseling to military personnel who have married women in the host countries. The resulting marital problems stem from the friction between two cultures.

If you are interested in this type of work, you should contact the military branch that interests you and inquire about civilian positions for social workers in foreign countries. You would be well advised to have your MSW, although they may consider an individual who has a BSW. Be prepared for the government scrutiny that any civilian receives when applying for a military position. If you are concerned about being stranded on a base without backup support, check out the bases to which you could be assigned. Find out how many social workers currently work there, and what the turnover rate has been in these jobs. Ask if you can contact a social worker who is currently working there, or—better yet—one who has just finished the job.

You may be interested in hospice work, which is a combination of a clinical and medical social worker. A hospice is a homelike setting for persons who are terminally ill. People go there to die, rather than in a hospital.

Your job, then, as a social worker is to help the patient and his family accept his approaching death. You do this by listening to them all and by helping them say their goodbyes so that no one is left with regrets. Of course, it also means being able to deal with death yourself. We all realize that people die; it is far harder to watch someone die—someone to whom you have grown attached, or someone who may seem too young. If you can handle your tasks with sensitivity and balance, you will be a welcome addition to this profession. There is great demand for social workers with the training (and, more important, the disposition) to work in this setting, particularly with the increasing threat of AIDS.

If you are interested in this work, spend your practicum in apprenticeship with another social worker at a hospice. Although your abilities and sensitivity are of more practical use, you would be wise to get your MSW degree. Read books by Elisabeth Kübler-Ross and other authors who are renowned for work with the terminally ill. Deal with your own "death anxiety" first, so that you can bring compassion—not fear—to the job.

Many social workers find their first job through Youth Services, which is a government agency funded by the United Way. Because it employs Bachelor level social workers (or even individuals with a Bachelor's degree in a related field), the pay is on the low end of the scale. It will be helpful if you like working with adolescents, since you will mainly work with them. You might also be involved in groups for runaways and other troubled youths, or you might be counseling teens who are having trouble with school. Once you are trained, you might be offering training in peer mediation. The advantage is that the work is challenging. The drawbacks are the pay and the need to work evenings or even weekends.

Some social workers work at the Travelers Aid Society. Originally, these workers assisted staff in hospitals and welfare offices to finance transients on their way home. For that reason they often worked in bus or train stations or at airports. Because of the shift in attention to the homeless population, social workers in this agency now focus 75 percent of their work on resettling the homeless. Most of their work is crisis-oriented and involves making referrals to other service agencies. Sometimes the Travelers Aid social worker uncovers abuse in the families she serves; although the abuse is reported, the social worker still works with the families to strengthen appropriate ties.

Like the clinical social worker but on a lesser scale, this social worker counsels some street people who remain in her community and still need resources and support to manage their lives. She is not unlike the medical and Human Services social workers who continually link these people to other community funds. It is her job to help them find food and shelter and to provide funds to go back "home," if they have one. The job is at the low end of the pay scale because it is an entry-level position, despite the sophisticated skills required. Because it is privately funded through donations and the United Way, it cannot afford to offer real pay incentives.

Travelers Aid work can be used as a stepping-stone to other jobs because the skills cultivated are easily transferable. The MSW is not required at this time.

Several jobs have been created to deal with the problem of abuse in families. Perinatal, neonatal, and pediatric social workers may find employment in day-care centers, community outreach programs, child welfare agencies, and family service agencies. These social workers receive extensive training working with children.

Social workers today are more sensitized to the problems of child abuse, but unfortunately are still constrained by the same forces: red tape and the courtroom. Emotional abuse, while every bit as painful as physical abuse, is very difficult to substantiate. Therefore, workers are not encouraged to take these cases to court.

Social workers (or at least their supervisors) are often reluctant to investigate charges of institutional abuse. Institutions are better able to hide their abuse; it takes a diligent social worker to uncover things that the institutions don't want uncovered. Not only that, but many of these institutions serve as DHS placement resources. If you shut them down, where will the kids go? The result of all these pressures is burnout. The child welfare worker knows the problems exist but is powerless to do much about them. What is worse, society still blames her for not doing more.

As public awareness of child abuse has grown, so has the need for social workers to testify in court. They have been used in the past as "lay witnesses," but more and more, they are being used as "expert witnesses," a classification that allows them greater latitude.

Another placement is with Intensive Family Preservation Services. The goal for these workers is to treat the whole family within its own environment. The idea behind it is to keep the children from being placed outside the home. Whatever it takes to keep the family intact, that becomes the social worker's job. For some, it means providing parenting skills and disciplinary techniques; for others, it might be helping set up a budget. You might have to settle a landlord dispute or help one of the parents find a job. Naturally, this kind of work is short-term and "labor-intensive," and it is oddly reminiscent of the jobs social workers used to do years ago, before specialization.

Social workers can work as therapeutic foster care therapists, considering both the foster care parents and the foster children as their clients. The agencies they work for may or may not have a Christian orientation.

Briefly, therapeutic foster care therapists divide their week counseling several families. The reason the children are in "therapeutic" foster care versus regular foster care is because they are having behavioral or emotional problems as a result of abuse and neglect.

You have to be able to connect with both the child and the foster parents, and at the same time maintain the right amount of professional distance to be able to provide each with constructive criticism.

Obviously since you actually go out to the foster homes to work, your schedule may vary from the regular eight-to-five workday. You may consider an erratic schedule either a good point or a disadvantage, depending on whether you yourself need structure and supervision to get your work done.

There are numerous therapeutic foster care agencies and opportunities to provide a number of services in addition to therapist: case management, intake coordinator, recruiting, training and certifying new foster parents, and supervising other therapists.

You may not have the time (or chance) to help every foster child in your care. Many move continuously through the system, going from home to home. Once they leave your assigned homes, they move on to new therapists. Sometimes you have to gear down your expectations (so as not to feel let down) and be ready to allow that child to move on. You just concentrate on what you can do to help.

I could have included this next job in the chapter on Administration because these managers do administrative work. The difference is that some social workers who are managers of specialized programs (such as Day Hospital where clients come daily for services, or Partial Hospitalization for more intensive work) are actually hired by other companies and contract for services with these agencies.

A company such as Horizon Mental Health Management of Lewisville, Texas, has contracts with many facilities throughout the United States and is always looking for new opportunities.

Your job as an administrator within these programs is much the same as explained in chapter 8. However, because you are hired by the management company, your allegiance is to them. Sometimes the regular staffs of the hospitals see you as an intruder and don't accept you as "one of them." Of course, you are not one of them because when the contract runs out or is terminated, you're out of a job.

The pay is above average ($33,000–$56,000) and the work rewarding, but because of the nature of contracts, employment is not stable. You may find yourself without a job should the company choose not to renew its contract, and should you choose not to move to another facility.

Mental Health Management facilities are always looking for new people, but you would be wise to get experience in mental-health settings before trying to market yourself to these management agencies. An MSW with licensure is expected.

Many people get their first experience in mental health by manning crisis hotlines. People with sensitivity and the ability not to panic are good candidates. They are trained on the job in handling crisis phone calls: learning resources to refer people to, and learning how to handle a person threatening suicide. People often find that this job, while very stressful, best prepares them for going into work as a therapist or case manager.

MOCS (mobile outreach crisis services) is the name of our mobile crisis intervention team. Most major cities have MOCS units available to go out into the community. They are made up of a psychiatrist, a registered nurse, and a clinical social worker (therapist). They make "wellness checks" if a client has not been seen in a long time or a relative has reason to believe the client is psychotic. Sometimes MOCS take the police along with them if the visit may prove dangerous.

MOCS also provide crisis services to clients in the community who for one reason or another can't get in to the mental-health center to get their medications. The team takes the medication out to them and sometimes provide therapy to get the client past the crisis before referring him for regular treatment at the local mental-health center.

This job is demanding, scary, fulfilling, and adventurous. No one can predict what the day's activities will include. The pay is average, depending on your position and years of experience, and the hours vary. But crisis intervention work is excellent preparation for any other social work job.

Other social workers who may practice the same skills as the clinical social worker operate in specialized fields such as substance-abuse or eating-disorder programs. They may be recovering themselves, but they nonetheless possess the educational background and experience to counsel people in these programs. Substance-abuse programs have their own special focus. Some advocate the use of antidepressants to treat the patient's underlying depression once the alcohol and drugs are removed. Other programs believe that reliance on drugs is part of the problem.

In eating-disorder groups, the social worker must not only possess good clinical skills but also be well versed in the subterfuges of eating-disordered clients. The anorexic or bulimic client dreads "getting fat" and fears giving the control of her eating patterns to the therapist. Working with resistant clients is exhausting work. The gains are few; the losses are substantial.

If you are interested in working in these specialized programs—and for some people it is personally rewarding, challenging work—I suggest you hire on first as an aide while you are still in school. You need the MSW degree, but the practical experience of working closely with clients on a day-to-day basis is invaluable.

The pay varies in this field, as do the specific tasks. If a program is privately funded, you stand to earn more money. Sometimes you can work in a clinical capacity, establishing your credentials so that you can then hire out as a consultant. As a consultant you can name your own salary.

Many of the jobs discussed in the proceeding chapters will hire BSWs. Often your supervisor will expect you to go on and get your MSW degree; some agencies even pay for you to do it.

Nonetheless, here are a few positions that will hire BSWs:

1. case managers
2. intake coordinators
3. Department of Human Services
4. probation and parole officers
5. crisis hotlines, crisis intervention teams
6. psychiatric techs
7. family planning clinics
8. Travelers Aid Society

In most of the jobs mentioned in this chapter, you must possess the ability to work with low-income people. It is not enough to "want" to help them; as traditional social workers find when working in low-income neighborhoods, those who need help resent being in that position. You must understand that people in less fortunate circumstances are not less human. And you, as the helper, are not more human.

When you work with people in different cultures, do not suffocate them with your culture. Our ways are not necessarily better, nor are they even helpful to some people. Respect other people's ways of life; don't impose your own ways on them. When you work with people who seem to lack control over their impulses, impose some restraint, if necessary. We all have our problems; we're never immune.

PART III

MAKING THE MOST OF YOUR SOCIAL WORK DEGREE

Mistakes You'll Survive

Let's look at some typical first weeks on a job. No matter that it isn't your dream job; it is important to learn how to behave on any job because you won't earn good references for your next job if you mess up on the first.

You don't have to be an inexperienced teenager to be unaware of on-the-job behavior. I was in my midtwenties and working as a social worker when I got clued in to some of my own misbehavior on the job. Back then, when work was slow or clients didn't keep appointments, I often had a block of free time. Most of the other social workers had similar free time, but whereas they chose to spend theirs in their offices, I sat with the receptionist, comparing notes on our weekends. Since I wasn't talking loudly, and I wasn't discussing clients' cases, I thought this behavior was acceptable. One day, a supervisor took me aside. She told me that although I behaved professionally in all other respects, the sitting in the lobby was hurting my image.

"How's that?" I asked. "I see my clients. I'm caught up on my paperwork, and I'm not talking about anyone."

"I'll tell you how it looks to other people," she said. "It looks as if you have nothing else to do so you sit out here gossiping."

"But I've done all my work," I objected.

"They don't know that," she said. "If you have nothing better to do with your time, read the professional journals. Volunteer to cover an admission or two, but either stay busy or stay out of sight."

Looking back on that incident now, I hate to think I needed someone to tell me that. So, to spare you some of the same embarrassment, let me share some thoughts on handling that first job or two. If I am now an expert, it's only because I've made mistakes.

On any job, you should spend more of your time listening than talking. You cannot figure out what your tasks are if you're trying to second-guess your boss. Let her talk. It's discourteous to interrupt, anyway.

Don't bring personal effects to the office. If you have a temporary job you only create a mess, and even in a private office you don't want to create the impression that you live there. Save the pictures of your boyfriend, girlfriend, or spouse for your bedroom. Clients don't need to know where your love interests lie.

If you choose to decorate your work space, use taste and good sense. Expensive knickknacks will only distract you from your job. If you spend time worrying about art objects on your desk, pack them up and take them home.

No matter how professional you are otherwise, don't make yourself visible in unproductive ways. Customers and clients don't like to discover that an employee is bored in his job. Leave your books at home if you can't keep your hands off them during work. Also, don't lounge around the reception area. You'll only invite criticism.

If you have some free time, catch up on your paperwork. If you are caught up, take advantage of the break by volunteering to help somewhere else.

When you first start working—no matter where it is—be careful of the alliances you make. Every office has cliques, and in the beginning you won't know who belongs to which one. It is best to be friendly with everyone, but making buddies (or worse, lovers) of your colleagues is asking for trouble. Try to keep your work separate from your personal life.

Speaking of your personal life, it has no place in the office. If you are too upset to work, either take the day off or explain to your boss—and only your boss—why you can't perform. No one needs to learn that your father has lost his job, or that you just broke up with your fiancée. If you are working with clients you are there to focus on their problems, not your own. Take care of your personal stuff on your own time.

Don't gossip—ever. It is unprofessional, and it reflects worse on you than on the one gossiped about.

If you hand in reports, be sure your writing is legible. People who have to type your reports and other social workers who have to rely on your written notes will be frustrated if they can't read them. In hospitals where documentation is essential for accreditation, administrators expect you to keep accurate and legible records. If you don't, they lose money and you are likely to be out of a job.

Wear appropriate clothing to your job. Don't dress provocatively or shabbily. Being careless of your appearance is discourteous to others who have to be in your company.

I'm sure I don't have to remind you to show up on time and in condition to work. Sporting a hangover, a two-day beard, or the clothes you wore the day before is no way to impress your supervisors.

Smoking rules are posted in most agencies. Respect the rules. In many facilities (particularly health settings) smoking is not allowed on the premises. Sneaking a smoke in the bathroom is not only frowned on; it is not tolerated.

Let's talk about "leave time." Most of you will receive a certain number of hours a month for sick leave or vacation time. Use your time wisely. Don't call in sick to go shopping at the mall. Murphy's Law states that "Whatever can go wrong will go wrong," so be aware that little lies can backfire. If you want to impress people with your dependability, then be dependable!

When you are fresh out of college you are typically full of ideas to "change the world." But problems crop up if you disagree with your colleagues or supervisors over your ideas. Often there are reasons why the old ways work better. Watch for a while to learn these ways. Offer suggestions when you have had time to see how things work at your agency. Don't embarrass your supervisor (or anyone else, for that matter) in a meeting where others will witness the verbal clash. Express your concerns privately to the person with whom you are in conflict. Don't go over a supervisor's head immediately; that strategy backfires more often than it works. Don't create the impression that you are difficult to work with; such comments become part of your "invisible file" at an agency. I said in an earlier chapter that there are times to take a stand and times to stand back. Learn to tell the difference.

Sometimes you will face conflicts of conscience. When Dwain was working as an aide in a nursing home years ago, he discovered that the private patients received preferential care over the welfare recipients. Even the food received was different. At the time the home was being investigated for those very practices. One of the investigators wanted to talk to Dwain about it. Should Dwain have admitted the preferential treatment, which would surely have meant losing his job? Should he have kept quiet and continued to work at a place that displayed unfair treatment? Or should he have kept quiet and tried himself to make up for the differences in treatment?

In such a predicament you have to weigh the pros and cons and decide whether your conscience will permit you to stay. If the pay is good or economic times are bad, you won't want to lose your job. In that case, don't bad-mouth your supervisors to salvage your conscience. If you work in an agency, support it—and that means not talking ill of any of its employees. If you are looking for another job, the worst thing you can do is badmouth your previous employer in an interview. The new agency will wonder what kind of personality conflict you got into and if you will get into similar difficulties again.

Lastly, don't take on more extracurricular activities than you can handle. It's all well and good to want to "fit in" quickly, but volunteering (and thus, overextending yourself) to host every party or cover every news event will wear you out. Take on only those tasks for which you have time. Set priorities so you end up doing the important things or the things for which you have talent.

When we start out in the world of work we all make mistakes. We can laugh about some of those mistakes later. Oddly enough, people never seem to learn from doing something right. They learn best from mistakes.

If you make a few mistakes, don't despair. As long as you learn from the experience, consider it a lesson in growing up. Fortunately, we never have to provide a history of our mistakes to people. We just live and learn, as the saying goes.

As social workers gain more authority and recognition, they face the possibility of more litigation. Just like doctors, social workers can be sued for mistakes and lapses in judgment.

But as the profession's stature grows, so will the compensation. Maybe by the time you're part of the workforce, this won't be an underpaid profession.

Don't sit around socializing in your spare time. Stay productive.

A Stepping-Stone to Other Jobs

The good part about having a social work background is that you can do so many other things as well—even things that don't fall into the category of social work. Social workers are often drawn to jobs requiring attention to detail and a great deal of resourcefulness. For those very reasons, social workers make good negotiators and arbitrators.

Negotiators work for companies (or are hired as consultants) to settle internal disputes as well as negotiate contracts with other businesses. The ordinary man on the street can now "rent" a negotiator to help him buy a car and secure the best deal possible. A negotiator doesn't need an MSW or even a BSW; all he or she needs are good negotiating skills. Good negotiating skills consist of 1) good listening skills, 2) good communication skills, and 3) a sensitivity to others (including a knowledge of nonverbal communication). Ideally, social workers should possess all these skills, given that their work is based on interaction with others.

Arbitrators are third-party negotiators who have the legal authority to solve disputes. People who come to arbitrators agree ahead of time to abide by the decision of the arbitrator (and also relinquish their say in negotiating a final decision). Courts often use an arbitrator (if the litigants are willing) to settle a dispute without the case coming to trial.

All you need to be an arbitrator is the right set of skills (as noted above). If you're interested in these two job opportunities, you might want to read *High Performance Through Negotiation* and *Coping Through Conflict Resolution and Peer Mediation*. Negotiating skills are certainly going to be in great demand. Even if you don't want to work as an arbitrator yourself, you could use the skills to train others.

Hospitals and mental-health centers are often turning to social workers to act as clinical directors or executive directors. Here's where your MSW pays off, though you won't necessarily be doing traditional social work tasks. As a clinical director, you may be responsible for overseeing your agency's psychologists as well as social workers. As an executive director, you'll be administering a budget and interacting with other agencies (and people) in the community. It is not essential to be a social worker to land the job, but your social work background will provide you with the skills to do these administrative jobs well.

Another thing you can do is teach. Not necessarily teaching social work, either. If you've accumulated enough hours in another subject (usually psychology or sociology), you may be eligible to teach those subjects in a community college. Social workers often make good psychology instructors because (1) they're attentive to detail (and can keep track of grades and other paperwork); (2) they like working with people; and (3) if they've done clinical work they know a lot about psychology anyway. So, just because you have your degree in social work, don't assume that's the only thing you'll ever be able to teach. Try a related field.

Social workers can also become good writers. Ann Hood, for example, was a social worker. She's written several well-received novels, including *Something Blue* and *Somewhere Off the Coast of Maine*. Needless to say, those books are not about social work. Why would social workers make good authors? For one reason, they have had a great deal of experience working with people. They should be familiar with people's actions and behaviors and the underlying reasons for them. They should also have a lot of stories, having seen much and done much as a social worker. You certainly don't have to be a social worker to write a good novel, but the experience of having been one won't hurt.

Lastly, social workers make great community leaders (no matter what the group) because they tend to be good organizers. Most social workers are resourceful, patient in the face of adversity, sensitive to others, and persistent—all good qualities to have in running any kind of organization.

Colleges Offering MSWs

ALABAMA
University of Alabama
School of Social Work
Box 870314
Tuscaloosa, AL 35487-0314
Lucinda Lee Roff, Dean
Phone: (205) 348-7027
Fax: (205) 348-9419

ARIZONA
Arizona State University
School of Social Work
Box 871802
Tempe, AZ 85287-1802
Emilia E. Martinez-Brawley, Dean
Phone: (602) 965-2795
Fax: (602) 965-5986

ARKANSAS
Univ of Arkansas Little Rock
School of Social Work
2801 South University
Little Rock, AR 72204
Howard M. Turney, Director
Phone: (501) 569-3240
Fax: (501) 569-3184

CALIFORNIA

California State University Fresno
Dept of Social Work Education
M/S 102
5310 Campus Drive
Fresno, CA 92740-8019
Vishu Visweswaran, Director
Phone: (209) 278–3992
Fax: (209) 278-7191

California State University Long Beach
Department of Social Work
1250 Bellflower Boulevard
Long Beach, CA 90840-0902
Jan Black, Interim Director
Phone: (562) 985-4616
Fax: (562) 985-5514

California State University Sacramento
Division of Social Work
6000 J Street
Sacramento, CA 95819-6090
Irving Berkowitz, Director
Phone: (916) 278-6943
Fax: (916) 278-7167

California State University San Bernardino
Department of Social Work
5500 University Parkway
San Bernardino, CA 92407
Teresa Morris, Director
Phone: (909) 880-5501
Fax: (909) 880-7029

Loma Linda University
Department of Social Work
Loma Linda, CA 92350
Beverly J. Buckles
Phone: (909) 478-8550
Fax: (909) 478-4450

San Diego State University
School of Social Work
5500 Campanile Drive
San Diego, CA 92182-4119
Anita S. Harbert, Director
Phone: (619) 594-6865
Fax: (619) 594-5991

San Francisco State University
School of Social Work
1600 Holloway Avenue
San Francisco, CA 94132
Robert G. Walker, Acting Director
Phone: (415) 338-1003
Fax: (415) 338-0591

San Jose State University
College of Social Work
1 Washington Square, Suite 215
San Jose, CA 95192-0124
Sylvia R. Andrew, Dean
Phone: (408) 924-5800
Fax: (408) 924-5892

University of California Berkeley
School of Social Welfare

120 Haviland Hall
Berkeley, CA 94720-7400
James Midgley, Dean
Phone: (510) 642-5039
Fax: (510) 643-6126

University of California Los Angeles
Department of Social Welfare
3250 Public Policy Building
Box 951656
Los Angeles, CA 90095-1656
James Lubben, Chair
Phone: (310) 825-2892
Fax: (310) 206-7564

University of Southern California
School of Social Work
MRF Bldg Rm 214
699 West 34 Street
Los Angeles, CA 90089-0411
Marilyn Flynn, Dean
Phone: (213)740-8311
Fax: (213) 740-0789

COLORADO
Colorado State University
Department of Social Work
127 Education Building
Fort Collins, CO 80523-1586
Ben P. Granger, Chair
Phone: (970) 491-6612
Fax: (970) 491-7280

University of Denver
Graduate School of Social Work
2148 South High Street
Denver, CO 80208-2886
Catherine F. Alter, Dean
Phone: (303) 871-2886
Fax: (303) 871-2845

CONNECTICUT
Southern Connecticut State University
Graduate Social Work Program
P. R. Lang Social Work Center
101 Farnham Avenue
New Haven, CT 06515
Elbert Siegel, Director
Phone: (203) 392-6560
Fax: (203) 392-6580

University of Connecticut
School of Social Work
1798 Asylum Avenue
West Hartford, CT 06117
Kay Davidson, Dean
Phone: (860) 570-9141
Fax: (860) 570-9139

DELAWARE
Delaware State University
Department of Social Work
1200 North DuPont Highway
Dover, DE 19901-2277
Jacquelynn Gorum, Dean

Phone: (302) 739-5175
Fax: (302) 739-5035

DISTRICT OF COLUMBIA
Catholic University of America
National Catholic School of Social Service
Washington, DC 20064
Sr. Ann Patrick Conrad, Dean
Phone: (202) 319-5454
Fax: (202) 319-5093

Gallaudet University
Department of Social Work
800 Florida Avenue NE
Washington, DC 20002-3695
Janet L Pray, Director
Phone: (202) 651-5160
Fax: (202) 651-5817

Howard University
School of Social Work
601 Howard Pl NW
Washington, DC 20059
Richard A. English, Dean
Phone: (202) 806-7300
Fax: (202) 387-4309

FLORIDA
Barry University
E. W. McDonnell School of Social Work
11300 NE Second Avenue
Miami, FL 33161
Stephen M. Holloway, Dean

Phone: (305) 899–3904
Fax: (305) 899-2973

Florida International University
School of Social Work
AC-1 Building Street 234
3000 NE 145th Street
North Miami, FL 33181
Max Rothman, Coordinator
Phone: (305) 919-5880
Fax: (305) 919-5313

Florida State University
School of Social Work
Tallahassee, FL 32306-2024
Dianne H. Montgomery, Dean
Phone: (904) 644-4752
Fax: (904) 644-8995

University of Central Florida
School of Social Work
P.O. Box 163358
Orlando, FL 32816
Ira Colby, Director
Phone: (407) 823-2114
Fax: (407) 823-5697

University of South Florida
School of Social Work
SOC 107
4202 East Fowler Avenue
Tampa, FL 33620-8100
Jean F. Amuso, Director

Phone: (813) 974-2063
Fax: (813) 974-4675

GEORGIA
Clark Atlanta University
School of Social Work
J.P. Brawley at Fair Street SW
Atlanta, GA 30314-4391
Dorcas Bowles, Dean
Phone: (404) 880-8548
Fax: (404) 880-6434

University of Georgia
School of Social Work
105 Tucker Hall
Athens, GA 30602
Bonnie Yegidis, Dean
Phone: (706) 542-5435
Fax: (706) 542-3282

HAWAII
University of Hawaii
School of Social Work
2500 Campus Rd
Honolulu, HI 96822
Patricia L Ewalt, Dean
Phone: (808) 956-6300
Fax: (808) 956-5964

IDAHO
Boise State University
School of Social Work

1910 University Drive
Boise, ID 83725
Juanita Hepler, Chair
Phone: (208) 385-3146
Fax: (208) 385-4291

ILLINOIS
Aurora University
School of Social Work
347 S Gladstone
Aurora, IL 60506-4892
Sandra Alcorn, Dean
Phone: (630) 844-5419
Fax: (630) 844-4923

Loyola University Chicago
School of Social Work
820 North Michigan Avenue
Chicago, IL 60611
Joseph A. Walsh, Dean
Phone: (312) 915-7005
Fax: (312) 915-7645

Southern Illinois University, Carbondale
School of Social Work
Quigley Hall
Carbondale, IL 62901-4329
Martin Tracy, Director
Phone: (618) 453-2243
Fax: (618) 453-1219

University of Chicago
School of Social Service Administration

969 East 60th Street
Chicago, IL 60637
Jeanne Marsh, Dean
Phone: (773) 702-1144
Fax: (773) 834-1582

University of Illinois Chicago
Jane Addams College of Social Work
1040 West Harrison Street, MC 309
Chicago, IL 60607-7134
Creasie Finney Hairston, Dean
Phone: (312) 996-3219
Fax: (312) 996-1802

University of Illinois, Urbana Champaign
School of Social Work
1207 West Oregon Street
Urbana, IL 61801
Jill Doner Kagle, Dean
Phone: (217) 333-2261
Fax: (217) 244-5220

INDIANA
Indiana University
School of Social Work
Education Social Work Building
902 West New York Street ES 4138
Indianapolis, In 46202-5156
Roberta R. Green, Dean
Phone: (317) 274-6705
Fax: (317) 274-8630

University of Southern Indiana

Department of Social Work
8600 University Boulevard
Evansville, In 47712
David Westhuis, Director
Phone: (812) 464-1843
Fax: (812) 464-1960

IOWA
University of Iowa
School of Social Work
308 North Hall
Iowa City, IA 52242-1223
Saloma Raheim, Interim Director
Phone: (319) 335-1250
Fax: (319) 335-1711

KANSAS
University of Kansas
School of Social Welfare
Twente Hall
Lawrence, KS 66045-2510
Ann Weick, Dean
Phone: (913) 864-4720
Fax: (913) 864-5277

KENTUCKY
University of Kentucky
College of Social Work
619 Patterson Office Tower
Lexington, KY 40506-0027
Kay Hoffman, Dean

Phone: (606) 257-6654
Fax: (606) 323-1030

University of Louisville
Kent School of Social Work
Louisville, KY 40292
Terry Singer, Dean
Phone: (502) 852-6402
Fax: (502) 852-0422

LOUISIANA

Louisiana State University
School of Social Work
Huey P. Long Field House
Baton Rouge, LA 70803
Kenneth I. Millar, Dean
Phone: (504) 388-1351
Fax: (504) 388-1357

Southern University
School of Social Work
6400 Press Drive
New Orleans, LA 70126
Millie M. Charles, Dean
Phone: (504) 286-5376
Fax: (504) 286-5387

Tulane University
School of Social Work
6823 Saint Charles Avenue
New Orleans, LA 70118-5672
Suzanne England, Dean

Phone: (504) 865-5314
Fax: (504) 862-8727

MAINE

University of Maine Orono
School of Social Work
5770 Annex C
Orono, ME 04469
Gail Werrbach, Director
Phone: (207) 581-2387
Fax: (207) 581-2396

University of New England
School of Social Work
Hills Beach Road
Biddeford, ME 04005
Elizabeth Ruff, Interim Director
Phone: (207) 283-0171
Fax: (207) 284-7633

MARYLAND

University of Maryland Baltimore
School of Social Work
Louis L. Kaplan Hall
525 West Redwood Street
Baltimore, MD 21201-1777
Jesse J. Harris, Dean
Phone: (410) 706-7794
Fax: (410) 706-0273

MASSACHUSETTS

Boston College

Graduate School of Social Work
McGuinn Hall
Chestnut Hill, MA 02167-3807
June Gary Hopps, Dean
Phone: (617) 552-4020
Fax: (617) 552-3199

Boston University
School of Social Work
264 Bay State Road
Boston, MA 02215
Wilma Peebles-Wilkins, Dean
Phone: (617) 353-3750
Fax: (617) 353-5612

Salem State College
School of Social Work
352 Lafayette Street
Salem, MA 01970
Donald P. Riley, Director
Phone: (978) 542-6629
Fax: (978) 542-6936

Simmons College
School of Social Work
51 Commonwealth Avenue
Boston, MA 02116-2307
Joseph M. Regan, Dean
Phone: (617) 521-3900
Fax: (617) 521-3980

Smith College
School for Social Work

Lilly Hall
Northampton, MA 01063
Anita Lightburn, Dean
Phone: (413) 585-7977
Fax: (413) 585-7994

Springfield College
School of Social Work
263 Alden Street
Springfield, MA 01109-3797
Francine J. Vecchiolla, Dean
Phone: (413) 788-2400
Fax: (413) 788-2412

MICHIGAN
Eastern Michigan University
Department of Social Work
King Hall, Room 411
Ypsilanti, MI 48197
Elvia Krajewski-Jaime, Director
Phone: (313) 487-0393
Fax: (313) 487-6832

Grand Valley State University
School of Social Work
25 Commerce Street SW
Grand Rapids, MI 49503
Rodney Mulder, Dean
Phone: (616) 771-6550
Fax: (616) 771-6570

Michigan State University
School of Social Work

254 Baker Hall
East Lansing, MI 48824-1118
John Herrick, Acting Director
Phone: (517) 353-7515
Fax: (517) 353-3038

University of Michigan
School of Social Work
Ann Arbor, MI 48109-1106
Paula Allen-Meares, Dean
Phone: (734) 764-5340
Fax: (734) 764-9954

Wayne State University
School of Social Work
201 Thompson Home
4756 Cass Avenue
Detroit, MI 48202
Leon W. Chestang, Dean
Phone: (313) 577-4400
Fax: (313) 577-6555

Western Michigan University
School of Social Work
Kalamazoo, MI 49008-5034
Philip Popple, Director
Phone: (616) 387-3170
Fax: (616) 387-3183

MINNESOTA
Augsburg College
Social Work Department
2211 Riverside Avenue

Minneapolis, MN 55454-1351
Glenda Dewberry Rooney, Chair
Phone: (612) 330-1189
Fax: (612) 330-1493

College of St. Catherine/University of St. Thomas
School of Social Work
Mail LOR 405
2115 Summit Avenue
Street Paul, MN 55105
Barbara W. Shank, Dean
Phone: (612) 962-5800
Fax: (612) 962-5819

University of Minnesota Duluth
Department of Social Work
220 Bohannon Hall
Duluth, MN 55812
Dennis Falk, Acting Director
Phone: (218) 726-7245
Fax: (218) 726-7073

University of Minnesota Twin Cities
School of Social Work
400 Ford Hall
224 Church Street SE
Minneapolis, MN 55455
Jean K. Quam, Director
Phone: (612) 624-5888
Fax: (612) 626-0395

MISSISSIPPI
Jackson State University

Graduate School of Social Work
3825 Ridgewood Road
Jackson, MS 39211
Gwendolyn Prater, Dean
Phone: (601) 987-4388
Fax: (601) 364-2396

University of Southern Mississippi
School of Social Work
Box 5114
Hattiesburg, MS 39406-5114
Earlie M. Washington, Director
Phone: (601) 266-4163
Fax: (601) 266-4165

Saint Louis University
School of Social Service
3550 Lindell Boulevard
Street Louis, MO 63103
Susan Tebb, Dean
Phone: (314) 977-2712
Fax: (314) 977-2731

MISSOURI
University of Missouri Columbia
School of Social Work
701 Clark Hall
Columbia, MO 65211
Charles Cowger, Director
Phone: (573) 882-6208
Fax: (573) 882-8926

Washington University

G W Brown School of Social Work
Campus Box 1196
1 Brookings Drive
Saint Louis, MO 63130-4899
Shanti K. Khinduka, Dean
Phone: (314) 935-6693
Fax: (314) 935-8511

NEBRASKA
University of Nebraska Omaha
School of Social Work
Annex 40
60th Street and Dodge Street
Omaha, NE 68182-0293
Sunny Andrews, Director
Phone: (402) 554-2793
Fax: (402) 554-3788

NEVADA
University of Nevada Reno
School of Social Work
Business Building, Room 525
Mail Stop 090
Reno, NV 89557-0068
Dean Pierce, Director
Phone: (702) 784-6542
Fax: (702) 784-4573

NEW JERSEY
Rutgers University
School of Social Work
536 George Street

New Brunswick, NJ 08903
Mary Edna Davidson, Dean
Phone: (732) 932-7253
Fax: (732) 932-8915

NEW MEXICO
New Mexico Highlands University
School of Social Work
Singer Hall, Room 205
Las Vegas, NM 87701
Alfredo Garcia, Dean
Phone: (505) 454-3593
Fax: (505) 454-3290

New Mexico State University
Department of Social Work
PO Box 30001, Dept 3SW
Las Cruces, NM 88003-8001
John Ronnau, Director
Phone: (505) 646-2143
Fax: (505) 646-4116

NEW YORK
Adelphi University
School of Social Work
Garden City, NY 11530
Roger Levin, Acting Dean
Phone: (516) 877-4354
Fax: (516) 877-4392

Columbia University
School of Social Work
622 West 113th Street

New York, NY 10025-7982
Ronald A. Feldman, Dean
Phone: (212) 854-5189
Fax: (212) 854-2975

Fordham University
Graduate School of Social Service
113 West 60th Street
New York, NY 10023-7479
Mary Ann Quaranta, Dean
Phone: (212) 636-6616
Fax: (212) 636-7876

Hunter College
School of Social Work
129 East 79th Street
New York, NY 10021
Bogart Leashore, Dean
Phone: (212) 452-7085
Fax: (212) 452-7150

New York University
S. M. Ehrenkranz School of Social Work
1 Washington Square North
New York, NY 10003
Thomas M. Meenaghan, Dean
Phone: (212) 998-5959
Fax: (212) 995-4172

Roberts Wesleyan College
Division of Social Work
2301 Westside Drive
Rochester, NY 14624

William R Descoteaux, Director
Phone: (716) 594-6410
Fax: (716) 594-6480

SUNY at Albany
School of Social Welfare
135 Western Avenue
Albany, NY 12222
Lynn Videka-Sherman, Dean
Phone: (518) 442-5324
Fax: (518) 442-5380

SUNY at Buffalo
School of Social Work
359 Baldy Hall
Buffalo, NY 14260-1050
Lawrence Shulman, Dean
Phone: (716) 645-3381
Fax: (716) 645-3883

SUNY at Stony Brook
School of Social Welfare
Health Sciences Center, Level 2, Room 093
Stony Brook, NY 11794
Frances L. Brisbane, Dean
Phone: (516) 444-2139
Fax: (516) 444-8908

Syracuse University
School of Social Work
Sims Hall
123 College Place
Syracuse, NY 13244-1230

William L Pollard, Dean
Phone: (315) 443-5550
Fax: (315) 443-5576

Yeshiva University
Wurzweiler School of Social Work
Belfer Hall
500 West 185th Street
New York, NY 10033
Sheldon R. Gelman, Dean
Phone: (212) 960-0820
Fax: (212) 960-0822

NORTH CAROLINA
East Carolina University
School of Social Work
Ragsdale Building Room 208A
Greenville, NC 27858
Gary R. Lowe, Dean
Phone: (919) 328-4208
Fax: (919) 328-4196

University of North Carolina Chapel Hill
School of Social Work
Tate Turner Kuralt Building, CB 3550
301 Pittsboro Street
Chapel Hill, NC 27599-3550
Richard L. Edwards, Dean
Phone: (919) 962-1225
Fax: (919) 962-0890

NORTH DAKOTA
University of North Dakota

Department of Social Work
Box 7135
Grand Forks, ND 58202-7135
G. Michael Jacobsen, Chairperson
Phone: (701) 777-2669
Fax: (701) 777-4257

OHIO
Case Western Reserve University
Mandel School of Applied Social Sciences
10900 Euclid Avenue
Cleveland, OH 44106-7164
Darlyne Bailey, Dean
Phone: (216) 368-2270
Fax: (216) 368-2850

Ohio State University
College of Social Work
1947 College Road
Columbus, OH 43210-1162
Tony Tripodi, Dean
Phone: (614) 292-5300
Fax: (614) 292-6940

University of Cincinnati
School of Social Work
PO Box 210208
Cincinnati, OH 45220
Philip Jackson, Director
Phone: (513) 556-4615
Fax: (513) 556-2077

OKLAHOMA
University of Oklahoma

School of Social Work
Rhyne Hall
Norman, OK 73019-0475
Julia M. Norlin, Director
Phone: (405) 325-2821
Fax: (405) 325-7072

OREGON
Portland State University
Graduate School of Social Work
P.O. Box 751
Portland, OR 97207-0751
James H. Ward, Dean
Phone: (503) 725-4712
Fax: (503) 725-5545

PENNSYLVANIA
Bryn Mawr College
Graduate School of Social Work and
   Social Research
300 Airdale Road
Bryn Mawr, PA 19010-1697
Ruth Mayden, Dean
Phone: (610) 520-2603
Fax: (610) 520-2655

Marywood University
School of Social Work
2300 Adams Avenue
Scranton, PA 18509
William H. Whitaker, Dean
Phone: (717) 348-6282
Fax: (717) 961-4742

Temple University
School of Social Administration
Ritter Hall Annex
13th Street and Cecil B. Moore Avenue
Philadelphia, PA 19122
Curtis A. Leonard, Dean
Phone: (215) 204-8623
Fax: (215) 204-9606

University of Pennsylvania
School of Social Work
3701 Locust Walk
Philadelphia, PA 19104-6214
Ira M. Schwartz, Dean
Phone: (215) 898-5541
Fax: (215) 573-2099

University of Pittsburgh
School of Social Work
2117 Cathedral of Learning
Pittsburgh, PA 15260
David E. Epperson, Dean
Phone: (412) 624-6304
Fax: (412) 624-6323

Widener University
Graduate Social Work Program
Center for Social Work Education
1 University Place
Chester, PA 19013
Paula T. Silver, Associate Dean
Phone: (610) 499-1153
Fax: (610) 499-4617

PUERTO RICO
University of Puerto Rico
Escuela Graduada de Trabajo Social
Decanato de Ciencias Sociales
PO Box 23345
San Juan, PR 00931-3345
Victor I. Garcia Toro, Director
Phone: (787) 764-0000
Fax: (787) 763-3725

RHODE ISLAND
Rhode Island College
School of Social Work
Providence, RI 02908
George D. Metrey, Dean
Phone: (401) 456-8042
Fax: (401) 456-8620

SOUTH CAROLINA
University of South Carolina
College of Social Work
Columbia, SC 29208
Frank B. Raymond III, Dean
Phone: (803) 777-5291
Fax: (803) 777-3498

TENNESSEE
University of Tennessee Knoxville
College of Social Work
109 Henson Hall
Knoxville, TN 37996-3333
Karen Sowers-Hoag, Dean

Phone: (423) 974-3176
Fax: (423) 974-4803

TEXAS

Our Lady of the Lake University
Worden School of Social Service
411 SW 24th Street
San Antonio, TX 78207-4689
Santos H. Hernandez, Dean
Phone: (210) 434-3969
Fax: (210) 431-4028

University of Houston
Graduate School of Social Work
Houston, TX 77204-4492
Karen A. Holmes, Dean
Phone: (713) 743-8085
Fax: (713) 743-3267

University of Texas Arlington
School of Social Work
Box 19129
Arlington, TX 76019
Richard L. Cole, Interim Dean
Phone: (817) 272-3946
Fax: (817) 272-3770

University of Texas, Austin
School of Social Work
Mail Code D3500
1925 San Jacinto Boulevard
Austin, TX 78712
Barbara White, Dean

Phone: (512) 471-1937
Fax: (512) 471-7268

UTAH
Brigham Young University
School of Social Work
221 Knight Mangum Building
PO Box 24472
Provo, UT 84602-4472
Kyle L. Pehrson, Director
Phone: (801) 378-3282
Fax: (801) 378-4049

University of Utah
Graduate School of Social Work
Social Work Building
Salt Lake City, UT 84112
Kay Dea, Dean
Phone: (801) 581-6192
Fax: (801) 585-3219

VERMONT
University of Vermont
Department of Social Work
228 Waterman Building
Burlington, VT 05405
Stanley L. Witkin, Chair
Phone: (802) 656-8800
Fax: (802) 656-8565

VIRGINIA
Norfolk State University

E. R. Strong School of Social Work
2401 Corprew Avenue
Norfolk, VA 23504
Moses Newsome Jr., Dean
Phone: (757) 683-8668
Fax: (757) 683-2556

Radford University
School of Social Work
Box 6958
Radford, VA 24142
Phone: (540) 831-5266
Fax: (540) 834-1142

Virginia Commonwealth University
School of Social Work
PO Box 842027
1001 West Franklin Street
Richmond, VA 23284-2027
Frank R. Baskind, Dean
Phone: (804) 828-1030
Fax: (804) 828-7541

WASHINGTON
Eastern Washington University
Inland Empire School of Social Work and Human
    Services
MS19 Senior Hall
526 Fifth Street
Cheney, WA 99004-2431
Michael L. Frumkin, Director
Phone: (509) 359-2283
Fax: (509) 359-6475

University of Washington
School of Social Work
4101 15th Avenue NE
Seattle, WA 98195-6299
Nancy R. Hooyman, Dean
Phone: (206) 685-1662
Fax: (206) 543-1228

Walla Walla College
Graduate School of Social Work
204 South College Avenue
College Place, WA 99324-1198
Standley L. Gellineau, Director
Phone: (509) 527-2590
Fax: (509) 527-2253

WEST VIRGINIA
West Virginia University
School of Social Work
P.O. Box 6830
Morgantown, WV 26506
Karen V. Harper, Dean
Phone: (304) 293-3501
Fax: (304) 293-5936

WISCONSIN
University of Wisconsin, Madison
School of Social Work
1350 University Avenue
Madison, WI 53706-1510
Mel Morgenbesser, Director
Phone: (608) 263-5612
Fax: (608) 263-3836

University of Wisconsin Milwaukee
School of Social Welfare
P.O. Box 786
Milwaukee, WI 53201
James A. Blackburn, Dean
Phone: (414) 229-4400
Fax: (414) 229-5311

Web Sites to Explore

National Association of Social Workers
http://www.socialworkers.org

Social work and social service jobs online:
http://www.gwbssw.wustl.edu

Social work access network:
http://www.sc.edu/swan/

The internet online career center:
http://www.occ.com/occ

For Further Reading

Compton, Beulah, and Galaway, Burt. *Social Work Processes*. Illinois: The Dorsey Press, 1989.

Doelling, Carol. *Social Work Career Development*. Washington, DC: NASW Press, Inc. 1997.

Germain, Carel, and Gitterman, Alex. *The Life Model of Social Work Practice*. New York: Columbia University Press, 1980.

Judson, Clara Ingram. *City Neighbor: The Story of Jane Addams*. New York: Charles Scribner's Sons, 1951.

McNeer, May, and Ward, Lynd. *Armed with Courage*. New York: Abington Press, 1957.

Peavy, Linda, and Smith, Ursula. *Dreams into Deeds*. New York: Charles Scribner's Sons, 1985.

Teare, R., and Sheafor, B. *Practice-Sensitive Social Work Education*. Alexandria, VA: Council on Social Work Education, 1995.

Index